Who Shot JFK?

Other Pocket Essentials by the same author:

Conspiracy Theories
The Rise of New Labour

Who Shot JFK?

ROBIN RAMSAY

POCKET ESSENTIALS

This edition published in 2007 by Pocket Essentials
P.O.Box 394, Harpenden, Herts, AL5 1XJ
www.pocketessentials.com
Series Editor: Nick Rennison
Index & Proofing : Richard Howard

ISBN 10: 1-84243-232-X
ISBN 13: 978-1-84243-232-7

2 4 6 8 10 9 7 5 3 1

Typeset by Avocet Typeset, Chilton, Aylesbury, Bucks
Printed and bound in Great Britain by J.H.Haynes Ltd, Sparkford, Somerset

Contents

Introduction

Many books about the Kennedy assassination don't offer a solution. Well, this one does. For those who don't want to wait for it, this book presents fairly recent evidence that JFK wasn't murdered by the CIA, or the Mafia, or the anti-Castro Cubans, or the military, or the Israeli secret service, Mossad, or the British royal family, or the KGB (all of whom have been touted as candidates, some more seriously than others), or a permutation of those, but by the most obvious candidate of all, JFK's vice president, Lyndon Baines Johnson. But in assassinology, as elsewhere, it is often more interesting to travel than it is to arrive.

Why Bother with this Old Stuff?

More than 15 years ago I was invited to talk to a group of Kennedy assassination enthusiasts in Liverpool, who called themselves Dallas 63. I had come to their attention because I had published articles on the assassination in the magazine I edit and publish, *Lobster*; and was just about the only person doing so in the UK at a point when major media interest in the assassination was at a pretty low ebb. I only knew one of the Dallas 63 group very slightly before I went and I discovered I was talking to people who knew more about the assassination than I did; or certainly knew more about particular areas than I did. For serious Kennedy assassination students almost invariably move into a specialism: the autopsy, the Dallas police, the motorcade, Officer Tippit, Cuba, CIA, ballistics etc etc.

I'm a generalist, interested in lots of areas, and my talk was a generalist's view of the event, surveying the various candidates as possible answers to the question, 'Who did it?' I thought then it was the Mafia: Jack Ruby's central role surely meant this. Recent new research has complicated things. My audience listened politely but, as soon as I finished and comments were invited, my talk was forgotten as they moved into their own areas and disappeared into relatively minor details, leaving me way behind.

Which is to say that the first thing a writer about to embark on this subject has to get past is the scale of it. The Kennedy assassination literature is now too vast to encompass: a thousand books, perhaps, over the last 40 years, a dozen or so journals, now defunct, two government reports and a mountain of supporting material, dozens of videos and DVDs, and God knows how many websites. Starting from scratch, working full-time, I guess it would take a year to get to grips with the basic material and, if we include in the picture the millions of declassified pages released by the government in the last two decades, it is now an impossible task to 'cover the field'. Some of the material is now so complex and so muddled as to be already virtually impenetrable. The medical/forensic evidence, to take the best example, is an absolute nightmare: it isn't even clear which of the putative autopsy photographs and X-rays are of JFK's head. (This is discussed in chapter 6.) To write even a small book about this subject, like this one, means writing while knowing you don't know enough.

Some of the Americans trying to handle the flood of government-generated material in this field suspect that the flood of information from the government is done to keep them busy – a belief recently partly confirmed as true. In his excellent book about the Anglo-American intelligence services in the Cold War, *The Hidden Hand* (London: John Murray, 2001), the historian Richard Aldrich reports:

> In 1998 officials prepared a report on the 'Operations Security Impact of Declassification Management within the Department of Defense', for the US Assistant Secretary of Defense... [the report] suggests that 'interesting declassified material' such as information about the assassination of John F. Kennedy could be released and even posted on the Internet as a 'diversion'. Newly released archives on such high profile subjects could be used to 'reduce the unrestrained public appetite for "secrets" by providing good faith distraction material'.

'Good faith distraction material'? George Orwell would have loved that!

The second major difficulty with writing (or reading) about the Kennedy assassination lies in these questions: why spend the time on something that happened long ago and which has no bearing on the modern world? These events in 1963 are irrelevant today as the world slides slowly down the pan. How important is a dead American president compared to, say, global warming or the power of the multinationals? Surely JFK's death should come a long way down the agenda of things worth pursuing? In some moods I feel this to be true but mostly I think that such a view underestimates both the *actual* historical significance of the Kennedy assassination and its *potential* political significance.

JFK's Historical Significance

Not only is there something intrinsically important about the murder of the president of the most powerful nation on earth, but the murder of *that* president, at *that* moment, makes it that much more significant; and the fact that his murder remains unsolved, with a cover-up lasting this long and so tenaciously defended, makes it more so.

The consensus view of Kennedy is that beneath the thin veneer of glamour – all that Camelot guff – he was just another politician, who did little of significance that would not have been done by Richard Nixon, had

Nixon, and not Kennedy, succeeded in stealing the 1960 election. The consensus view might continue that this is not only specifically true in JFK's case but also necessarily true because individuals cannot much affect the workings of the system. Wider economic and political forces will prevail. Individuals are actors, performing the script written by the money. This determinist view is obviously true in general but individuals – Lenin, Trotsky, Mandela, Hitler, Churchill, Roosevelt, Thatcher, for example (and the list could be extended) – can have a big impact. There are also individuals who *might* have made a big impact, had they lived. In America the dead Kennedys, John and Robert, and Martin Luther King were such individuals. Indeed, many of the Kennedy assassination researchers believe that it was precisely *because* they were going to make an impact – the wrong impact for parts of the system – that they were killed.

I don't have room here for a detailed account of the debate about who Kennedy really was and I don't think we need it. On any view, by the standards of 1950s America, JFK was an unusual president. In his 1961 book *The Presidential Papers*, Norman Mailer tried to portray JFK as the first existential president (whatever that meant!), a hipster. As it turned out, in some senses, Mailer didn't even get close. For JFK was a sexual compulsive who used his status to try to have sex with anything (female) that moved; and he was smoking dope and doing cocaine. Funky times at the White House!

Funkier times than Norman Mailer dared to imagine in 1961!

But Kennedy was also rather more than that. He was the president who knew he owed his 1960 election victory to the Mafia and was willing to share a woman – Judith Campbell – with one of the Mob's leaders. The Frank Sinatra-Sammy Davis Jnr-Dean Martin-Peter Lawford 'rat pack', in which there is a revival of interest[4], contained a junior member, Lawford, who had married into the Kennedy family, and Sinatra, its leader, openly socialised with Mob figures. Which is perhaps saying nothing more than this: things were afoot in the early 1960s. Smoking dope and doing cocaine and banging starlets in the White House pool is a big jump from the Doris Day version of America served up to the world in American popular culture of the 1950s, and symbolised in its political culture by outgoing Republican President Dwight D. Eisenhower. There is a big shift going on in that transition period between Eisenhower and what is now thought as 'the sixties'. Kennedy was part of that, as well as a symbol of it, but he was also a symbol of the power of the Mafia in those days. And the Mafia thought they'd helped get him there and he owed them.

Even Eisenhower could feel the winds rising. War-hero, war-leader, soldier and Republican, Dwight Eisenhower had used a televised farewell address to the American people not to say, 'I'm off to play golf and God bless America', but to warn them of the dangers presented by the American 'military-industrial complex' – the Pentagon and its vast hinterland of arms manufacturers.

Into this context arrived Kennedy, who talked the conventional Cold War–Soviet menace talk when he had to before the election, but who, after the failed invasion of Cuba at the Bay of Pigs and the subsequent Cuban Missile Crisis, went off the rails as far as the military-industrial complex was concerned. He did a deal with Khrushchev and promised to leave Cuba alone; he began trying to wind down the CIA's army of anti-Castro Cubans; he signed the Test Ban Treaty; he was preparing to allow the Italian Communist Party into a coalition government in Italy, something the CIA had worked to prevent since 1945, spending hundreds of millions of dollars and utterly corrupting Italian society in the process; he was planning to cut US defence spending abroad to reduce the US balance of payments deficit; and he wanted to begin pulling the US out of Vietnam. These are not the actions of a Cold Warrior. The Cuban Missile Crisis had scared the politicians involved in it.[5]

In a sense, the debate about who Kennedy was is easily solved: there were two 'Kennedys'. The Cold Warrior Kennedy who got elected changed – or dropped his conservative cover – after the Cuban Missile Crisis and became a liberal Democrat.

Perhaps most significant of all, Kennedy wanted out of the then rapidly expanding war in Vietnam. The military-industrial-intelligence complex and the political right saw Kennedy's deal with Khrushchev over Cuba as retreat in the Caribbean and his plans for Vietnam as retreat in the Far East. The military-industrial complex wanted war in Vietnam as part of what they saw as the ongoing Cold War struggle with communism; it was just a bonus that, in pursuing the war, they stood to make a lot of money and have good careers. Whether or not we try to locate the assassination conspiracy in this milieu, and many of the researchers do, we can agree that Kennedy was going up against the military-industrial complex on almost all fronts – the forces his predecessor had warned against.[6] When the scale of what Kennedy was thinking of doing is understood, it is very tempting to see his assassination in terms of Kennedy stepping too far out of line and the system getting rid of him.

Oliver Stone

The idea that Kennedy was too radical for the military-industrial complex is the thesis behind the two motion pictures about the case: the dull 1973 version, *Executive Action*, which starred Burt Lancaster, and Oliver Stone's *JFK*. Stone emphasised Vietnam: Kennedy was shot to stop withdrawal from Vietnam. This is the thesis most closely associated with the late L. Fletcher Prouty, former US Air Force colonel, who had a remarkable book, *The Secret Team,* published in America in 1973. Prouty was a really important insider, not only the US

Air Force's liaison officer with the CIA's covert operations in the 1950s, but someone who had also been in charge of presidential security. As former liaison with the CIA, Prouty had watched the growth of the agency's covert operations which he saw as corrupting the US military. As a former presidential security officer, Prouty looked at the events that day in Dallas and saw the *absence* of presidential security. As Prouty pointed out, the absence of security is all you need to arrange. Prouty implied, but never quite stated, that the US Secret Service had to be part of the plot. This never seemed likely to me but some recent research, which I discuss below, makes it less implausible than before. Unfortunately for Prouty his extraordinary book got buried under the Watergate scandal and was barely noticed at the time.[7]

That the publisher of the Pocket Essentials series thought this book worth commissioning we owe to Oliver Stone's movie which, though barking loudly up the wrong tree in the view of virtually all the Kennedy researchers, rekindled interest in the assassination when major factual TV documentaries and hundreds of books had not. I enjoyed *JFK* a lot but, like most people interested in the assassination, was irritated that Stone chose to portray the 1968 attempt by New Orleans District Attorney, Jim Garrison, to prosecute Clay Shaw. Few of the Kennedy researchers think Clay Shaw had anything to do with the assassination, fascinating figure though he turned out to be when Garrison dragged him into the light. In retrospect it is obvious that a mainstream, narrative filmmaker like Stone would choose this way into the assassination: it is the one aspect of the events since 1963 which is dramatic. Its 'story line' was a little guy fighting against the system. It even featured a Hollywood cliché, the crusading district attorney. Looked at like that, the story wrote itself. And however misconceived it was, Garrison's prosecution of Clay Shaw was the sole crack taken at the assassination by the American judicial system.[8]

The Potential Political Significance of Kennedy's Death

Before parts of JFK's skull bounced onto the boot of the presidential limousine that day in Dallas, the broad mass of Americans – make that *white* Americans – still believed what their government told them. Now they don't. No doubt many factors have contributed to this, most obviously the war in Vietnam, whose consequences ripped through American society in the 1960s and 1970s. But there, at the beginnings of America's belief that the government tells lies, was Kennedy's death – and the collapse of the government's version of it. That the government was manifestly lying about the biggest domestic political story of the time was hard to ignore.[9] This is one of those instances where the old adage that the truth is always subversive looks plausible.

But the Kennedy assassination is also the greatest and

most complex whodunnit of the last century; the biggest source of official paper on the activities of the American state; and the best route into the post-JFK era, from Vietnam, through Watergate and subsequent revelations. It is also the most striking example of a research effort in a Western democracy by private citizens, supported by neither of the main political parties and none of the state's bureaucracies (many of which, indeed, have done their best to frustrate it) and none of the major media (ditto).[10]

This shows one of the many paradoxes of the United States. On the one hand, the land of the brave and the home of the free, in which we have this activity by its citizens. On the other, a nation ruled by a political elite, which either permits the assassination of its leaders, or is in some way constrained from investigating their deaths. For all three of the major assassinations of the 1970s – JFK, RFK and Martin Luther King – were 'solved' without serious investigation, by attributing the deaths to patsies. This is the subversive potential of the subject: here is a modern industrialised society, the most powerful nation on earth, in which the three most important figures of a generation on the mainstream liberal-left were assassinated in a five-year period and there has not been a serious investigation into one of the deaths. If we are to pick at a scab on the hide of the elephant, we might as well pick at the biggest one. This is where the most official effort has gone into holding the line.

Notes

1. I nearly wrote 'Kennedy assassination buffs' but most Kennedy assassination researchers and students hate the word. Personally, I'm a 'Kennedy assassination buff'.

2. Two good starting points for JFK assassination information on the Web are <http://jfkresearch.free-homepage.com/links1.htm> and <http://www.jfk-online.com/jfklinks.html>.

3. It is now generally accepted that the Mob helped Kennedy steal a very close election. A search on Google for 'JFK + 1960 election + Mafia' in May 2007, as I was rewriting this book, produced 65,000 hits, many of them responses to, or commentaries on, the Seymour Hersh book *The Dark Side of Camelot* which contains the most readily accessible information on the 'theft'. See for example <www.time.com/time/magazine/1997/dom/97 1117/cover3.html>. Or see an interview with Hersh in *Atlantic Monthly* at <www.theatlantic. com/unbound/bookauth/shint.htm> where Hersh states, *inter alia*: 'The FBI produced a report for the Attorney General saying that the election had been stolen in Illinois.' There is also a nice summary of the election-fixing evidence in Sally Denton and Roger Morris, *The Money and the Power: The Making of Las Vegas and its Hold on America, 1947–2000* (New York: Alfred Knopf, 2001), chapter 12.

4. There was a 2001 remake of the 'rat pack' movie, *Ocean's Eleven* with George Clooney et al, a book, Shawn Levy's *Rat Pack Confidential* (London: Fourth Estate, 1998), and, as I write, a musical show called *The Rat Pack* is touring Britain. Given what we now know about the personal behaviour of Messrs Sinatra, Lawford and, to a lesser extent, Martin, 'rat' is appropriate.

5. The most striking interpretation of Kennedy as a left-liberal is in Donald Gibson, *Battling Wall Street* (New York: Sheridan Square, 1994).

L. Fletcher Prouty (see note 7 below) believed but couldn't prove that Eisenhower's warning about the military-industrial complex was Eisenhower's response to having his plans to cool the Cold War kiboshed by that complex. Prouty believed – and thinks that Eisenhower knew – that the shooting down of the U-2 plane piloted by Gary Powers, which collapsed Eisenhower's talks with the Soviet Union, was arranged by the CIA precisely to end the talks.

Stephen M. Birmingham – not the American popular writer of that name – contacted me and pointed out that Kennedy was also going up against the military-industrial complex in proposing a co-operative approach to space exploration with the Soviets. He has written:

John F. Kennedy's lasting desire regarding the manned lunar landing program is recorded in

National Security Action Memoranda 271 (a document kept secret for almost 20 years) in which he boldly called for the development of a program of substantial co-operation with the Soviet Union in matters relating to outer space, including collaboration in lunar landing programs; which he authorised and signed on November 12, 1963 – ten days before his dreadful assassination in Dallas. Yet to this very day its full significance is glossed over by the mass media and historians alike. Instead, they much prefer to centre on his now almost sacred May 25, 1961, speech, in which he first inspired so many Americans to reach for the moon.

From <http://www.birmo.co.uk/jfk/work_in_progress/index.htm>. At that address there is a detailed discussion of NSAM271.

6. The areas of Kennedy's conflict with the military-industrial-complex are described in great detail in Peter Dale Scott's essay, 'The Death of Kennedy, Vietnam, and Cuba' in *The Assassinations,* ed. Scott, Hoch and Stetler, (Harmondsworth: Penguin Books, 1978). If you have hitherto accepted the Kennedy-was-just-like-Johnson view, this Scott essay will be a revelation. The assumption that there was continuity between JFK's Vietnam policies and those of his successor, LBJ, lives on. The former chairman of the British Joint Intelligence Committee, Sir Percy Cradock, repeats this in his *Know Your Enemy: How the*

Joint Intelligence Committee Saw the World (London: John Murray, 2002) p. 195. Declassified papers on JFK's plans to withdraw from Vietnam can be seen at <http://www.historymatters.com/vietnam1963.htm>.

Two excellent recent books on the US military-industrial complex are James Carroll, *House of War* (Boston: Houghton Mifflin, 2006) and Ismael Hossein-Zadeh, *The Political Economy of U.S. Militarism* (New York: Palgrave Macmillan, 2006). The Carroll book covers the entire post-war period and conveys a very strong sense of what JFK was going up against; Hossein-Zadeh concentrates on more recent events, notably the recent American invasion of Iraq.

7. Prouty's *The Secret Team* is now available as a part of a CD-ROM of his collected writing from <http://www.prouty.org/cdrom.html>.

In Oliver Stone's movie Prouty is played by Donald Sutherland – 'just call me "Mr X"' – in the one really misjudged scene in the film.

8. The subtitle of Jim Garrison's 1988 account of this, *On the Trail of the Assassins*, is 'One man's quest to solve the murder that shook the world'. What a pitch!

9. In a piece originally published in the spring 2001 edition of *The Wilson Quarterly*, Max Holland accepts that the JFK assassination did have the effect of increasing American cynicism about the govern-

ment but with the spin that this was the fault of Jim Garrison's prosecution/persecution of Clay Shaw in New Orleans; and, because Garrison was conned by some Soviet-inspired disinformation about Clay Shaw, the KGB created that popular disaffection in the United States from the late 1960s onwards. He wants us to accept this syllogism:

- America was undermined by corrosive doubt created by the JFK assassination
- Garrison was at the heart of that
- Garrison was running Soviet disinformation
- Therefore... the Soviets undermined America.

10. On the role of media see Jerry Policoff, 'The Media and the Murder of John Kennedy' in *The Assassinations*, eds. Scott, Hoch and Stetler (Harmondsworth; Penguin, 1978). *The New York Times* and *Washington Post* had been thoroughly compromised by their association with the US military-intelligence complex, especially the CIA.

The Greatest Hoax

'And it was the greatest hoax that has ever been perpetuated...'
Richard Nixon's view of the Warren Commission, carried
by Reuters, 28 February 2002, reporting some of the
latest transcriptions of recordings of Richard Nixon made
in the White House during his presidency.

The official, government version of the assassination was
that lone assassin, oddball, ex-Marine, self-proclaimed
Marxist and defector to the Soviet Union – and how
weird was that in 1963? – Lee Harvey Oswald, shot
Kennedy from his place of employment, the Texas Book
Depository, which overlooked the route of the parade
Kennedy took through Dallas that day. He did it for
reasons unknown, but which probably owed much to his
personal inadequacies and jealousy of the charismatic
young president. Another wannabe getting his 15
minutes of fame, perhaps. According to the official
version, having shot Kennedy, he left his clapped-out,
dirt-cheap, WW1 surplus rifle with inaccurate sights,
ran down to the canteen in the warehouse and got a
Coke from the machine in time to be sitting there to be

confronted by a Dallas policeman investigating the shooting. Identified as an employee of the building, Oswald was ignored by the police and wandered out, caught a bus, went home, shot a Dallas policeman and sneaked into the movies without paying. Oswald was then arrested by the Dallas police and shot the next day, in the police station, by Jack Ruby, the owner of a strip club in the town. Incoming President Johnson set up a commission of inquiry, chaired by Chief Justice Earl Warren and stuffed with the great and the good – including Allen Dulles, erstwhile Director of the CIA, whom the dead president had fired. The Warren Commission, as it became known, after its inquiry, published a report stating that Oswald had done it alone.

The Commission's verdict was a lie, a deception, baloney – and insulting baloney at that. They didn't even do a good job on the deception. The politicians, the military and the intelligence services had been getting away with so much since 1945, they had the major media so totally co-opted into the Cold War crusade against the Soviet Union, that the Commission's members didn't think it would matter that their report was nonsense: they thought the *schmucks* would buy whatever was served up to them.

Thinking About the Assassination

If you think about the assassination from the point of view of those who organised it, it seems obvious that it must have been planned as a double murder: kill Kennedy and then leave behind a dead Oswald, the Marxist defector, the pro-Castro loner, as the 'assassin'. Dallas law enforcement would be presented with a crime *and* its solution, and noone would need to do much poking around. The signs of this scenario are obvious. There were the ridiculous fabricated photos of 'Oswald' posing with a rifle and holding left-wing newspapers. (Oswald's head had been stuck on pictures of someone else's body.) There was Oswald's rifle, allegedly found in the Book Depository, and a number of incidents before the shooting in which someone pretending to be Oswald was heard making anti-Castro noises and threats against JFK.

But the creation of the dead assassin Oswald went wrong and he survived to get himself arrested. It seems likely that he was supposed to die 'resisting arrest' – a not uncommon event in the United States in those days. But, confronted by the Dallas police in a cinema, Oswald may have saved his life by having the wit to shout out, 'I am not resisting arrest', in front of the dozen or so people in for the afternoon matinee. Oswald knew what the score was. One of the few things he said while in custody which was recorded was his statement to the media as he was being taken through the Dallas police station: 'I'm just the patsy'. Of more than a day's worth of interrogation by police and FBI, only a handful of scrappy notes by Dallas Police Chief Fritz – a few dozen words – have emerged.[1] The absence of a detailed record of what Oswald said while in police custody is one of the many striking facts in which the Warren Commission was uninterested.

With Oswald alive and in the hands of the police, the conspirators had a problem: how to kill Oswald with the attention of the world's media on him? Who could get at Oswald in police captivity? Step forward Jack Ruby, the Chicago Mob's police liaison officer in Dallas, friend of the boys in blue, a familiar face in the station, who could get into the building in those circumstances.

Jack Ruby

Ruby's role is significant, for Ruby is visible around the assassination. Dallas journalist Seth Kantor talked to Ruby – whom he knew, Ruby being a well-known figure in town – at the Parkland Hospital after Kennedy's body had been driven there after the shooting.[2] The Warren Commission simply ignored Kantor, saying he made a mistake. Ruby was also at the first press conference after the assassination given by the Dallas County District Attorney, Henry Wade, the man who ordinarily would be in charge of the investigation of the shooting. Briefing the press on what they knew about Oswald, Wade made what might have been a serious error, describing Oswald as being a member of the Free Cuba Committee, one of the CIA-funded, anti-Castro groups. 'Fair Play Cuba,' said a voice at the back of the conference. It was Jack Ruby, the Mob's man in Dallas, steering Wade and the press towards Oswald's one-man branch of the Fair Play for Cuba Committee. Noone seems to have thought it surprising that a local mobster would know this! Ruby then hung around the Dallas police station for several hours before turning up the next day and shooting Oswald, live on TV. Ruby has to be one of the conspiracy's action men on the ground, managing the situation – the one readily identifiable member of the assassination conspiracy at the scene.

Ruby looks like the key to the puzzle but he didn't much interest the early critical researchers. They chose to concentrate on Oswald and discovered that while he was officially portrayed as a leftist loner – reading Marx, defecting to the Soviet Union, publicly campaigning for Castro upon his return to the United States – this was just part of the picture. His military service had intelligence fingerprints all over it (reading Marx and learning Russian in the Marines?); his defection was a phoney; he was connected to the CIA and, upon his return from the Soviet Union, to the CIA-funded, anti-Castro Cubans; and he was well known to the local FBI. Oswald created a Fair Play for Cuba Committee (FPCC) branch in New Orleans which consisted solely of him and whose address was in a building full of the CIA's *anti*-Castro people. Though we cannot prove it, this FPCC branch was a phoney, set-up either to attract, and so identify for the FBI, other Castro sympathisers; or, perhaps, to discredit the national FPCC; or simply to create a 'legend' or cover-story for Oswald for some other purpose.[3]

Having uncovered this other, unofficial, intelligence-linked Oswald, many of the researchers concluded that the conspiracy had to involve the US government or state – its intelligence services or its military – at some level. (Who was organising the cover-up? they asked. The government, of course.) Many thought it would prove to be the CIA. This assumption was also made by elements within the British secret service at the time. Anthony Cavendish served in MI6 before becoming a banker. He was a lifelong friend of Maurice Oldfield, who became the chief of MI6, and of George Kennedy Young, MI6 vice chief. I asked Cavendish some years ago what his circle had thought when they heard of the assassination. Who did they think had done it? Why, the CIA, of course. Others thought it was maybe the agency's clients, the anti-Castro Cubans, who hated Kennedy for, as they saw it, selling out Cuba, and with whom Oswald, or someone pretending to be Oswald, had been working in the months before the assassination. (In so far as there is a consensus view among the JFK researchers on whodunnit, it would certainly involve the anti-Castro Cubans.)

Advance Knowledge: The Murder Conspiracy Was Leaky

There is an obvious, major difficulty with the assumption that the assassination was the work of some elements in the American state. Had it been the work of a state organisation – the CIA, say – why get rid of Kennedy in that way? Why ambush him in daylight as if it was the Wild West? Shooting from long-range at a moving target, even one moving as slowly as the presidential limousine did that day, is risky. The shots might miss and the would-be conspirators might be pursued by a vengeful president with all the powers of the state. (Many of the shots fired at Kennedy *did* miss. Six or seven shots were fired at the car: at least two each struck Kennedy and Texas Governor Connally, one missed and slightly injured a bystander and one struck the presidential limousine.) More telling still: if the assassination conspiracy was the work of some state organisation, why was it so leaky? We may presume universal incompetence, or Murphy's law, that what can go wrong will go wrong but would a state organisation planning to kill the commander-in-chief – the absolutely number one, big no-no – create a plot as leaky as this one was? For four people of whom we know had advance knowledge of the assassination: Joseph Milteer, a minor but apparently wealthy figure on the far-right, a junkie stripper named Rose Cheramie, a minor intelligence officer named Richard Nagell and a minor criminal and anti-Castro activist, John Martino.

Milteer was bugged in Miami by a police informant a couple of weeks before the assassination, talking of a plan to kill Kennedy with a rifle from a tall building, which was 'in the working'. Milteer also presciently noted that after the shooting, '…They will pick someone up within hours afterwards… just to throw the public off.'[4] Informed of the tape by the Miami police, the Secret Service, tasked with protecting the president, did *not* interview Milteer.[5]

The second person with advance knowledge of the assassination was Richard Case Nagell who, over many years, in confusing and elusive dribs and drabs, claimed that he knew Oswald, knew of the assassination plan, suspected he was about to get embroiled in it, and got himself into the safest place he could think of – jail. Two months before the assassination Nagell walked into a bank, fired two shots at the ceiling and waited for the police.[6]

On 20 November 1963, three days before the shooting, Lt. Francis Fruge of the Louisiana State Police went to Moosa Memorial Hospital in Eunice. The hospital had a junkie on its hands who was going into heroin withdrawal. (This was a good deal less common then than it is now.) This was Rose Cheramie, real name Melba Christine Marcades, who had been admitted to hospital after being injured by a car. At the hospital, Fruge was later to tell the House Select Committee on Assassinations in 1977, Cheramie told him her story. She had been en route from Florida to Dallas with two men who looked Cuban or Italian. All three were part of a drug-smuggling operation but the two men told her that they were going to kill the president in Dallas in just a few days. Cheramie was a courier of funds for heroin which was coming in through the port of Galveston,

Texas. But the three of them fell out and the two men dumped her. While hitchhiking she was hit by a car, the driver of which took her to the hospital.

Furthermore, according to a psychiatrist, Dr Victor Weiss, who talked to her after the assassination when she was admitted to hospital, Cheramie '… told him that she knew both Ruby and Oswald and had seen them sitting together on occasions at Ruby's club'; that she was acting as a drug courier for Ruby (Lt. Fruge later confirmed that she had worked as a stripper for Ruby); and that Ruby was part of the plot to kill the president – something, let us not forget, that is pretty obvious from his behaviour that day in Dallas.

On 25 November, after what Cheramie had predicted had indeed taken place, Fruge went back to interview her again in hospital, heard a more detailed version of the original story and, in the subsequent days, found that much of her story checked out. Lt. Fruge's boss rang Captain Fritz of the Dallas police to relay all this, to be told by Fritz that they weren't interested. By this time the decision had been taken in Washington that Oswald was going to be the lone assassin.[7]

Cheramie's banal little story is of low-level organised crime: the junkie courier going to pick up smack for Jack Ruby, the Mob's guy in Dallas. Bad-a-bing![8] Whether we regard this as significant or not, there are only two possibilities: either the Oswald assassination conspiracy was being gossiped about or there was another assassination conspiracy which was being

gossiped about.[9] Either way, Milteer and Cheramie –
and even Nagell and Martino[10] – are a long way down
the pecking order from anybody likely to be involved
in anything resembling a professional job by, say, the
CIA.

Looked at from the Jack Ruby end of the event,
shooting at Kennedy from long-range is the work of
people who cannot get closer to do it. Dealey Plaza as
the site was determined by the fact that Oswald worked
in a building there on the route of the motorcade and so
could plausibly be framed as the shooter.

In Washington the only concern was damage limita-
tion and information control. Cut off any inquiries,
wrap the whole thing up and, in effect, accept the
picture the conspirators had so incompetently arranged:
dead president, dead assassin. For some of the politicians
this was motivated by anxiety that the assassination
might have been the work of the Soviet Union or its
Cuban proxy. This belief was encouraged by a campaign
immediately after the assassination to sell the idea that
the shooting was the work of Castro – and thus, by
extension, the Soviet Union.[11] But there is an irony
here, because the effect of the Castro-did-it stories was
the opposite of that intended: rather than spur the
administration to take vengeful action against Cuba –
basically, support a second invasion – the alleged Cuban
connection encouraged the impulse to terminate
inquiries. The Cuban Missile Crisis was still fresh in the
memory in Washington and another showdown with the

Soviets over Cuba was feared rather than sought. Although the official word from the CIA was that neither Castro nor the Soviets had been involved, incoming president Lyndon Baines Johnson used the possibility that Castro did it to twist arms, shut down other bodies seeking to investigate the shooting, and run the lone assassin verdict.[12] With Oswald dead, the state, now headed by the new president Lyndon Johnson, knew that it needed a piece of impressive official bullshit to endorse the only *politically* safe story: that Oswald alone killed Kennedy. This wasn't even concealed. J. Edgar Hoover told LBJ's assistant Walter Jenkins: 'The thing I am concerned about, and so is Mr Katzenbach [the Deputy Attorney General] is having something issued so we can convince the public that Oswald is the real assassin.'

A memo on 25 November from Nicholas Katzenbach to LBJ's chief domestic assistant, Bill Moyers, began thus:

It is important that all of the facts surrounding President Kennedy's Assassination be made public in such a way which will satisfy people in the United States and abroad that all of the facts have been told and that a statement to this effect be made now:

1. The public must be satisfied that Oswald was the assassin; that he did not have confederates who are still at large; and that the evidence was such that he would have been convicted at trial.

Katenbach's statement ended thus: 'We need something to head off public speculation or Congressional hearings of the wrong sort.'

There was some urgency in Washington to get the event shut down. Texas law enforcement officials who were inclined to investigate the shooting as part of a conspiracy – probably, in their view, a communist conspiracy; they had discovered the 'Marxist' Oswald – were leaned on by the FBI to drop the idea on 24 and 25 November. In Washington, Senator Eastland was proposing to call hearings on the subject of Oswald-as-communist before the committee he chaired, the Internal Security Subcommittee. On 28 November a congressman proposed a Joint Congressional Committee to conduct an investigation. Two days later President Johnson announced the formation of the Warren Commission, killing the other congressional initiatives.[13] LBJ's first thought was of a Texas investigation which he could control. The Washington insiders didn't want that, presumably because they feared that it couldn't be controlled, or wouldn't be believed, and possibly because they feared the Texans would run their Oswald-communist theory which, as Katzenbach's 25 November memo discussed previously shows, was high on the list of things Washington *didn't* want airing. Katzenbach wrote, *inter alia*:

> Speculation about Oswald's motivation ought to be cut off, and we should have some basis for rebutting the

thought that it was a Communist conspiracy or (as the Iron Curtain press is saying) a right-wing conspiracy to blame it on the Communists. Unfortunately the facts on Oswald seem too pat – too obvious (Marxist, Cuba, Russian wife etc). The Dallas police have put out statements on the Communist conspiracy theory, and it was they who were in charge when he was shot and thus silenced…

This memo illustrates perfectly the utter lack of interest in 'the truth'. LBJ's phonecalls during this period were recorded and we can now read transcripts of what he was saying. In none of the conversations he was having in the first few days after the event does he, or those he was talking to, express any interest in 'the truth'. In his memo Katzenbach shows that he was suspicious of the Oswald story being a set-up – it was 'too pat', he wrote – but he wanted a cover-up anyway.

As the links between Oswald and various bureaucracies – the FBI and the CIA in particular – were revealed in the years following the murder, it became clear that these bureaucracies had reasons to cover things up *whether or not* they had been involved in the shooting. Oswald's name popping up in the files of the CIA, FBI, Naval Intelligence and God knows where else was the ordure hitting the air circulation device and, faced with embarrassment, bureaucracies, and especially those kinds of bureaucracies, go into cover-up mode automatically. In retrospect, it is blindingly obvious that the one thing all the intelligence bureaucracies would do is hit the shredders and start putting out disinformation about

Oswald and their links with him. The bureaucracies of the American state – FBI, CIA et al – all agreed that it would serve none of them to have all this dragged out into the light. When Oswald's name surfaced, people in the FBI and CIA knew that their organisations had links to him which they wanted buried.

Discussing these links in detail is beyond the scope of this book but just consider the following: investigated even half seriously, Oswald would lead back to the CIA's then still officially secret anti-Castro operations being run in Miami and the CIA's anti-Soviet operations in Mexico City.[14] There was his false defection for starters, probably – but not yet certainly, to my knowledge – a CIA operation. (The CIA ran other false defectors into the Soviet Union and the KGB ran false defectors at the Americans in the Great Game of spying.) There were his links with George de Mohrenschildt and the other 'white' Russians in the Dallas area, amongst whom Oswald was deposited on his return from the Soviet Union. This whole episode is very odd indeed. Where does the Marxist former defector go? To a group of wealthy 'white' – i.e. anti-Soviet – Russian expatriates in the far right's major stronghold, Dallas. In his testimony to the Warren Commission, George de Mohrenschildt, who seems to have been baby-sitting Oswald in this period, called those 'white' Russians in Dallas, 'Solidarists'. And what are Solidarists? Members or supporters of NTS, an anti-Soviet group which had been run since the end of the Second World War, first by the

British MI6 and then, after 1956, by the CIA. Put it this way: if you had to define a group who would be *least* likely to adopt a Marxist former defector, it might be an anti-Soviet group of rich Russian exiles in Dallas, supporters of a group run by the CIA. Oswald was met on his arrival back in the US from the Soviet Union by a man from a CIA front group and was resettled among personnel/supporters of a CIA operation.

The FBI were embarrassed at several levels. Given Oswald's role as the designated hitter, they hadn't kept a close enough eye on him and were afraid they would be blamed for the assassination. J. Edgar Hoover was then under considerable pressure to resign and make way for a younger, less communist-obsessed man. Yet, irony of ironies, here was a presidential assassination apparently carried out by that rarest of rarities, an American Marxist defector to the Soviet Union – and right under the noses of the great red hunters, the FBI. It is also extremely likely, but not yet proven, that the FBI had been using Oswald as part of their Cointelpro – intelligence-gathering and disruption – operations against the Fair Play for Cuba Committee, although Freedom of Information requests have failed to turn up a single page on FBI Cointelpro operations against that organisation. Oswald, we may assume, was working as a low-level informant for the FBI and probably as an agent provocateur, tasked to set up a phoney Fair Play for Cuba Committee, a honey-trap for the local left. His curious behaviour in New Orleans – his I-am-a-Marxist radio talk; his arrest for giving out hands-off Cuba leaflets (an event created with a group of *anti*-Castro Cubans); his contacting the various American left groups; his creation of a Fair Play for Cuba branch at the address of the office of the violently *anti*-Castro former FBI agent Guy Banister – is all Oswald creating an identity for himself as a lefty, pro-Castro activist while, in fact, working for somebody else, most probably the FBI, perhaps at arms-length, through Guy Banister. There is quite a lot of evidence now on the FBI's use of former agents, such as Banister, in deniable operations.

In the end it suited the whole political-military-intelligence system, the US political establishment and, for reasons still unexplained, the Kennedy family, to go with the 'lone assassin' explanation. It was the only safe verdict.[15] In the long conversation referred to in note 12 at the end of this chapter, in which LBJ bullied and cajoled Senator Russell into sitting on the Warren Commission, the one thing never mentioned is 'the truth'. Politicians simply aren't interested in 'the truth', except when it can be used to assist their aims: getting or retaining power and damaging their opponents' chance of getting or retaining power. In the Kennedy assassination literature there is an almost total lack of interest in 'the truth' from his professional colleagues in the Democratic Party, from the justice system, or from the Kennedy family. 'The truth' simply didn't make it onto the agenda. Kennedy's death and the existence of an alleged assassin were simply political problems to be solved or exploited.

The Warren Commission

Incoming President LBJ twisted the arm of former Chief Justice Earl Warren to head the inquiry and a panel of the great and good was pressed into service. One of them was Allen Dulles, fired as head of the CIA by Kennedy after the failed attempt by the CIA to depose Castro. *Cuba again.*

Teams of lawyers were hired to go through the motions: not to investigate the crime but to use the evidence provided by the FBI to write a report showing that the assassin was Oswald, alone. The Commission members, the politicians, didn't attend most of the hearings. The Commission presumed that noone would read its report anyway. Allen Dulles, Commission member, famously said: 'But nobody reads. Don't believe people read in this country. There will be a few professors that will read the record... The public will read very little.'[16] The Warren Report was duly published, hailed (unread, no doubt) by the media, and that should have been that.

But it wasn't: the plan failed. The botched assassination was now the subject of a botched whitewash. The Warren Report's authors and commissioners didn't realise that there were people in the US who were savvy enough and sceptical enough about the government to analyse the report, to go through the evidence – beginning by providing an index to the 26 volumes of evidence (which the government had failed to do) – and see that the official story was nonsense.

That the Warren Report failed to sedate America wasn't really the fault of its creators. The material the report's authors were working with was just too messy and awkward to stuff neatly back into the cupboard. The 'evidence' framing Oswald might have been adequate for a dead Oswald, an open-and-shut case in the hands of the Dallas police, in the then obscurity of Texas, but it was not designed to withstand scrutiny. Had it come to trial, any half-decent lawyer would have reduced the frame to tatters. There was no decent evidence linking Oswald to the event. The physical evidence, a palm-print found on a cardboard box on the sixth floor of the book depository, was explicable: Oswald worked in the building, moving boxes. The alleged Oswald palm-print on the rifle allegedly found at the 'sniper's nest' was dubious in the extreme and the rifle was a dud with inaccurate sights which could never have done the job. (The best shots in the FBI came nowhere near being able to replicate Oswald's alleged shooting feat, using Oswald's alleged rifle or any other, more adequate rifle.) No eyewitnesses linked him with the shooting. The photographs showing Oswald posing with the rifle, which he claimed were faked, would have been examined and shown to be such. The various sightings of 'the second Oswald' would have been examined. And so forth. It was crudely done – just enough to provide the set dressing for the dead president/dead assassin scenario.

And there was the little matter of Oswald being shot on television by a Dallas gangster. Ruby was the Chicago

Mob's man in Dallas, paying-off the police, a middle-manager in organised crime. Hard though the Warren Commission tried to ignore this fact, to fudge Ruby's biography, and to pretend he wasn't a gangster, it was impossible to conceal.[17]

When the little group of people with doubts about the official verdict began to pick at the loose ends, the official version began unravelling immediately. Between 1964 and 1967 a series of books appeared, taking the official version to pieces: Joachim Joesten's *Oswald: Assassin or Fall-guy?* and Thomas Buchanan's *Who Killed Kennedy?* in 1964; Sylvan Fox's *The Unanswered Questions about President Kennedy's Assassination* in 1965; Mark Lane's *Rush to Judgement,* Edward Epstein's *Inquest,* Richard Popkin's *The Second Oswald* and Josiah Thompson's *Six Seconds in Dallas,* all in 1966; and Harold Weisberg's *Whitewash* and Sylvia Meagher's *Accessories After the Fact* in 1967.[18] Of these it was the Epstein and Lane books which got the attention of the media.

Notes

1. Photographs of the four pages of hand-written, abbreviated notes taken by Dallas Police Chief Captain Fritz are at <http://www.jfk-info.com/fritztit.htm>. If these are an accurate account of the main points, Oswald – no dummy, he – said almost nothing of consequence and was waiting for a lawyer.

2. There is a photograph of the back of a man at Parkland Hospital who looks remarkably like Jack Ruby on the rear cover of the pamphlet *Forgive My Grief III* by Penn Jones Jnr, (Midlothian, Texas; self-published 1969; reprinted 1976). There is an interesting 1975 profile of Ruby, 'Who was Jack Ruby?' by Gary Cartwright at <http://www.texasmonthly.com/archive/ruby/ruby.1.php.> It includes the following:

> He didn't drink or smoke. He was violently opposed to drugs, though he maintained his own high energy level by popping Preludin – an upper – and it was rumored that he operated a personal clearing house for Mob drug runners. He was involved in shady financial schemes, and the IRS was on his back. A swindler who called himself Harry Sinclair Jr. told Secret Service agents that Ruby backed him in a bet-and-run operation. Ruby supplied cash and introduced Sinclair to likely victims. (H. L. Hunt was supposed to have been one.) If Sinclair won, he'd collect; if he lost, he'd write a hot check and split. Ruby got 40 per cent of the action...

3. Oswald's links to the CIA are discussed in detail by former intelligence officer, John Newman, in his *Oswald and the CIA* (New York: Carroll and Graf, 1995). There are no Freedom of Information documents available on the FBI's Cointelpro operation

against the Fair Play for Cuba Committee. To my knowledge there is no evidence that there *was* an FBI Cointelpro operation against the FPCC, but since there was a Cointelpro against much of the rest of the American left of the period, it is assumed there was such an operation and that its files have been suppressed. There is a large collection of Cointelpro documents and other information at <http://www.derechos.net/paulwolf/Cointelpro>.

4. Anthony Summers, *The Kennedy Conspiracy* (London: Warner Books, 1998) pp. 308–9. This is an update of his 1980 *Conspiracy*. The Milteer material is in all the versions of Summers' book.

5. At <http://mcadams.posc.mu.edu/milteer.htm> there is a lengthy and sceptical account of Milteer which tries but fails to obscure the fact that Milteer did say what he said. This is a section of one of the best JFK sites, even though it is utterly hostile to the critics of the Warren Commission. For its acerbic view of the incompetence and sheer sloppiness of many of the critics, it is very useful. And interesting. And frequently funny. For example at <http://mcadams.posc.mu.edu/rashomon.htm> they list 61 (!) people who have been variously named as the shooters.

6. Nagell's tantalising and ultimately incomprehensible story is in Dick Russell's account of him, *The Man Who Knew Too Much* (New York: Carroll and Graf,

1992). All 700 plus pages of it. The book defies
summary.

7. This is taken from the long and fascinating 'Rose
   Cheramie: How She Predicted the JFK Assassination' by Jim DiEugenio, to be found at <http://
   www.webcom.com/ctka/probeframes.htm.>
   There is another interesting take on Cheramie by
   the British researcher Chris Mills, 'Rambling Rose'
   at <alt.conspiracy.jfk.moderated>. Cheramie was
   murdered in 1965.

8. Ruby's strip club, The Carousel, was not that dissim-
   ilar to the Bad-a-Bing! in the TV series *The Sopranos*,
   though Ruby wasn't as far up the ladder as Tony
   Soprano. The account of Ruby, albeit mostly
   rumour, in the *Texas Monthly* profile referred to in
   note 2, depicts a milieu similar to that of the Mafia
   portrayed in *The Sopranos*.

9. This second thought may remind the reader of the
   wonderful scene in volume one of the Wilson/Shea
   Illuminatus Trilogy, in which several assassination
   teams squabble over who gets the best shooting
   position on the grassy knoll. That there might have
   been more than one JFK assassination conspiracy is
   possible. A man using the name Harry Dean, a self-
   styled former CIA and FBI agent, has claimed that
   he had infiltrated such a plot by members of the far-
   right John Birch Society. Dean has never been taken
   seriously by the Kennedy researchers, though I am
   not sure why. His account is included in Robert

Cutler and WR Morris, *Alias Oswald* (Manchester, Maine: GKG Partners, 1985), which also includes a photograph of him.

10. Martino's advance knowledge – or, more accurately, Martino's widow's account of Martino's advance knowledge – is discussed in Larry Hancock's very good *Someone Would Have Talked* (Southlake, Texas: JFK Lancer Productions, 2006).

11. This is discussed in detail in Peter Dale Scott, *Deep Politics II* (Skokie, Illinois: Green Archive Publications, 1995).

12. In Noel Twyman's *Bloody Treason* (Rancho Santa Fe, California: Laurel Publishing, 1977) – I am grateful to Tony Frewin for this – there is a transcription of a tape recorded phone call on 29 November between Johnson and senior Democratic Senator Richard Russell, in the course of which LBJ repeatedly uses the Castro/Soviet danger threat to persuade the extremely reluctant Russell to sit on the Warren Commission. I saw the following on the Net but have been unable to find its source. This is apparently an excerpt from a 26 November 1963 memo from the then Texas Attorney General Wagoner Carr:

> 'Mr. Fortas informed me that he has been assigned to co-ordinate the FBI, Department of Justice and Texas Attorney General's efforts regarding the assassination of President Kennedy.

Abe Fortas was Bobby Baker's lawyer and a (crooked) friend of LBJ whom LBJ later appointed to the Supreme Court – from which position he was forced to resign in 1969. (Baker is discussed later, chapter 5.) This appears to be an intermediary attempt by LBJ to control the investigation. His initial idea was to have a Texas investigation. He seems to have come round to a Presidential Commission when confronted by the determination of a number of Senators to have a Senate inquiry. When he failed to dissuade them of this idea he was forced to create a Presidential Commission, something he had opposed initially. The idea of the Presidential Commission was first mooted to LBJ by Eugene Rostow, via Johnson aide Bill Moyers and reinforced by *New York Times* journalist Joseph Alsop. See Donald Gibson, *The Kennedy Assassination Cover-up* (Huntingdon, NY: Nova Science Publishers, Inc., 2000), pp. 54–66, which includes a transcript of the Alsop-Johnson phonecall during which Alsop floated the commission idea.

13. The manoeuvrings around this have been widely discussed in the literature. The most recent account I read was in Gibson (see note 12).

14. The CIA officer in charge of the agency's liaison with the Warren Commission was James Angleton, the head of CIA Counter Intelligence. A group of his people had been running operations against the Soviet Embassy in Mexico City in which Oswald, or

someone calling himself Oswald (or both) were embroiled. This has been discussed in great detail by Peter Dale Scot in *Deep Politics II.* (See note 11.) I presume Angleton was appointed in part to ensure this material never made the agenda.

15. Just as it suited the same political establishment to try to suppress the investigation into the Bobby Baker scandal in 1963. Baker led to LBJ. In the end it was delayed long enough not to damage Johnson and Baker didn't grass on LBJ. This is discussed later in chapter 5.

16. Only a thousand sets of the 26 volumes of evidence collected by the Warren Commission were initially printed. One, happily, is in the library of the University of Hull where I stumbled over it in 1976. I was the first person to take out most of the volumes, more than a decade after they had been purchased. Whether by incompetence, haste or design, the evidence was assembled in a chaotic mess.

17. When asked why he had done it, Ruby said, with a straight face, that he'd done it to spare Jackie Kennedy the ordeal of a trial of Oswald! The Warren Commission had to work hard to not investigate Ruby. On this see David Scheim, *Contract on America: The Mafia Murder of President John F. Kennedy* (New York: Shapolsky Publishers, 1988), especially chapter 14. This has also been published as *The Mafia Killed President Kennedy.* On the details of Ruby's

career see Peter Dale Scott, *Deep Politics and the Death of JFK* (London: University of California Press, 1993), chapters 8 and 9.

18. A reasonable introduction to the major books in the Kennedy literature is <http://spot.acorn.net/jfkplace/09/fp.back_issues/17th_Issue/biblio_alph.html>

Way Down Yonder in New Orleans

Things began speeding up in 1967. Partly it was the cumulative effect of the work being done by the researchers: the Lane and Epstein books which got the media attention, chiefly, and others of the period. It was also partly the political context: the war in Vietnam was expanding and there was a steady procession of coffins bringing young men – mostly black young men – back to their home towns. The opposition to the war was growing. The war *was* coming home and the Kennedy assassination was still a live issue.

By 1967, the Warren Commission Report had been utterly trashed but no-one was any closer to finding out whodunnit. By 1967, everybody – the CIA, anti-Castro Cubans, pro-Castro Cubans, the FBI, the military, the oil industry, the KGB, LBJ, the Mafia or combinations of them – had been proposed as the culprits. At the heart of these early explorations was the question, *Cui bono?* (Who benefits?) which provided the rough and ready way to a hypothesis with which to look at the material. From Kennedy's death, unfortunately, almost everybody benefited: all of those listed above, various Latin

American dictators, the Vietnam war lobby, and even the Italian right, threatened by Kennedy's willingness to tolerate the Italian communists.[1] The only proposed candidates who manifestly *didn't* benefit were the Soviets and Fidel Castro, who lost the president who had done the secret deal with them on Cuba and pledged no invasion.

In 1967, Jim Garrison, the District Attorney of New Orleans (played by Kevin Costner in Oliver Stone's movie *JFK*) enters the story.[2] Oswald had been in New Orleans for a while, dickering with the *anti*-Castro Cubans while pretending to be *pro*-Castro. In 1963, Garrison's office had pursued one of these connections to their patch, Oswald's links to the fascinating character David Ferrie. A commercial pilot who had been fired for being gay, a putative priest in a tiny Catholic sect, anti-Castro activist, and a gofer for the Louisiana Mob boss, Carlos Marcello, Ferrie was one of several exotic creatures upon whom this story threw the spotlight. But, by the time his office had made inquiries about Ferrie, Garrison found that the FBI, to whom his office's work was referred, was not interested. (Lt. Fruge with his story about Rose Cheramie had the same experience.) The decision to shut down inquiries and go with Oswald as the 'lone assassination' had already been taken in Washington and new leads were the last thing that the FBI wanted. On his own account, Garrison shrugged – 'What do you expect from the Feds?' – went back to work and forgot about the assassination until 1966 when

Louisiana senator Russell Long told him that he didn't believe the Warren Report's version. This was no little thing Long was doing: no senior US politician had then raised a head above the parapet to announce his or her scepticism at this stage. His interest aroused, Garrison acquired a set of the Warren evidence and the Report, began reading the material, saw how weak the Warren Report was and decided to have a second look on the quiet at the lead his office had investigated in 1963.

Garrison duly persuaded himself that he had stumbled on the assassination conspiracy. I write 'persuaded himself' because it is now difficult to read accounts of this and not wonder what on earth Garrison thought he was doing, because he didn't have a case against the man he eventually charged, Clay Shaw, a patrician, gay businessman, some time playwright and aesthete, a regular on local TV, well known in the city for his efforts to conserve New Orleans' historic quarter. A less likely JFK conspirator it would be difficult to imagine.[3]

There is a gay dimension to the Kennedy assassination, although most researchers are reluctant to go near it in these PC times. Clay Shaw, the man Garrison accused, and David Ferrie, whom Garrison would also have charged had he not committed suicide (or been 'suicided'), were gay and moved in the same circle. There is a 1955 picture of Ferrie in the role of a commander in the Civil Air Patrol – akin, perhaps, to an air force version of the British Sea Scouts – with a group of youths, one of whom is Lee Harvey Oswald.[4] I think

Jack Ruby was a gay man in the closet. One of the people to whom Garrison talked in his inquiry was a New Orleans lawyer, Dean Andrews, who described Clay Shaw, under his alias Clem Bertrand, hiring him to help some 'gay Mexican kids' who were in trouble with the police. With these 'gay kids' was Oswald. Or so says Andrews.[5] Rose Cheramie, the junkie courier who predicted the assassination, is reported to have said of Ruby and Oswald: 'Them two queer sons-of-a-bitches. They've been shacking up for years.' Garrison's route into his 'JFK conspiracy in New Orleans' was via this gay network, linking Ferrie, Shaw and (possibly) Oswald. Garrison thought he had stumbled on the Kennedy assassination but it is more likely he stumbled on the New Orleans gay subculture.

Even in his own account of all this, *On the Trail of the Assassins*, in which everything is given the best possible gloss and none of his critics' points are presented, Garrison still doesn't seem to me to make even the beginning of a case against Shaw. Garrison's defenders – and there are some, notably Jim DiEugenio, Lisa Pease and, most recently, Professor Joan Mellen – will reply that Shaw was a CIA agent of some kind. This is true, though his known activities on behalf of the agency were slight: he was one of hundreds of American businessmen who, in the 1950s, reported back to the agency on what they had seen on their foreign travels.

The weakness of Garrison's case wasn't manifested until the trial itself and his investigation, producing headlines in the media, attracted some of the people already researching the case. Their input into his investigation, added to some of the information produced by his staff's investigation, accelerated the spread and availability of materials on the case – good and bad, reliable and unreliable. In the long run, the most significant thing about the case was that Garrison got access to the now famous Zapruder film, the home movie of the shooting. For the first time some American citizens, in a court room in New Orleans, got to see Kennedy's head jerking back and exploding in a pink halo of blood and brains as the bullet – or bullets – *that couldn't be Oswald's* hit it from the front.[6] Though Garrison's prosecution of Clay Shaw failed, the fact that it took place at all did much to persuade American public opinion that the Warren Report was not the end of the story.[7] It was Garrison who was seen and heard accusing the CIA and various other people – he never quite fixed on the other members of the cast – of assassinating the president and he *was* the district attorney of a major US city. The context helped: it was Garrison's good fortune to be making charges about the CIA at a time when the first big public exposures of CIA covert operations in US domestic politics were taking place in the mass media after initial exposure in the magazine *Ramparts* and it had become impossible for the establishment media and the politicians to say, 'This couldn't possibly happen.'

Garrison's critics are unclear why Garrison did what he did. Publicity seeking? The district attorney is an elected official, a politician, after all. Incompetence? *Worse?* In his book *Contract on America* (New York: Shapolsky Publishers, 1988) David Scheim noted, as others had before him, that among the various candidates he considered for the role of JFK conspirators, Garrison did not include organised crime. And he knew of the links: one of his leading candidates, David Ferrie, worked for Carlos Marcello, who was Mob boss of Garrison's patch. And, as District Attorney, he must have been quite acutely aware of the Mob's activities in his jurisdiction. Scheim invites the reader to conclude from his selection of the evidence that Garrison probably ran his investigation in part as a favour to his friends in the Mob; that Garrison, as district attorney and later as a judge, was working for the Mob; that his investigation was, in effect and intent, disinformation.[8]

I don't think it is likely that Garrison's inquiry *per se* was *deliberate* disinformation but his inquiry did generate one significant piece of disinformation which has dogged the case ever since: the Permindex story, the most significant in a series of disinformation projects created using the assassination.

A Digression about Disinformation

The first, and potentially the most dangerous disinformation project based on the shooting, was the attempt to persuade the US administration in the immediate aftermath of the assassination that Oswald was working for the Soviet bloc, either directly for the Soviets or for Cuba.[9] This communist conspiracy theory was being run by the Dallas police[10] and also by a Nicaraguan double agent who told a Mexico City CIA officer on 25 November that he had seen Oswald recruited to kill Kennedy inside the Cuban embassy in Mexico City.[11] The Dallas police may have believed the story as their initial investigation of Oswald turned up the 'left-wing' Oswald; the Nicaraguan agent was simply lying, though at whose behest isn't clear.

The second disinformation project we know of occurred in 1964 when the KGB paid a New York publisher, Carl Marzani, to publish Joachim Joesten's *Assassin or Fall-guy?*[12] This had little impact and it was buried by the appearance of the first two major assaults on the Warren Commission verdict, the books by Epstein and Lane.

The third disinformation project was the publication of a book by the French intelligence service, *Farewell America* by 'James Hepburn'. This attributed the affair to the CIA and the oil industry, I seem to remember. (My copy was lent to a JFK buff about 20 years ago and never returned.)[13] This achieved some notoriety within the JFK research community, mainly because, although many rumours about it circulated, it was hard to get hold of. My memory of it says that it contained nothing of substance – demonstrating, if nothing else, that in 1967 the French intelligence service didn't know who had done it – and it is now referred to in the literature only in the contexts of disinformation or interesting ephemera.

The fourth was the leaking of the claim that JFK was killed by the assassination team created by the Mob and the CIA to kill Castro, which had been 'turned' by Castro and pointed back at JFK. This was apparently done to distract attention away from Garrison's focus on the CIA.[14]

The fifth disinformation project around the case was Soviet disinformation about Clay Shaw, whom Garrison prosecuted for the assassination. Shaw was a director of the World Trade Centre in New Orleans and was brought into a similar project in Italy, involving a company called Permindex (Permanent Industrial Exhibitions) which proposed to create a network of World Trade Centres, all propagandising for American business. Around these bare facts a story was created in which all these companies were CIA fronts for covert operations and assassinations, in which Permindex had been involved in trying to assassinate General de Gaulle and had then killed JFK. This story was planted on a Soviet-sympathising Italian newspaper. It was then picked up by a left-wing magazine in New York and a magazine in Canada and thence made its way to the Garrison investigation. And Garrison believed it without checking it. His 1988 book, *On the Trail of the Assassins*, carries a couple of pages on Permindex in which he quotes only the Canadian and Italian versions of the story.[15] Parts of this Permindex story – itself disinformation – were then picked up and used to form the centre piece of the most famous and most durable piece of disinformation generated by the case, the *Nomenclature of an Assassination Cabal* by 'William Torbitt', better known as the Torbitt Memorandum. 'Torbitt' took Garrison's inquiry into the *CIA's* links to the assassination and converted them into a story about the *FBI's* responsibility for the assassination. (This, in my view, tells us that the author/s of Torbitt were working for the CIA, trying to diminish the 'Garrison effect'.) At the beginning of the first chapter, 'Torbitt' tells us that the assassination was the work of the FBI and the Defense Intelligence Agency, who jointly ran 'the Control Group'. These two agencies ran another *really* secret agency, the Defense Industrial Security Command (DISC). Clay Shaw, David Ferrie et al, previously identified as CIA, were in fact DISC. Because it was 'underground' and because it was full of interesting and authentic-sounding bits and pieces, Torbitt was 'sexy'. However, as soon as I began trying to check the few citations in it, they proved to be useless: either they didn't exist, were impossible to get, or, when tracked down, didn't say what 'Torbitt' said they did. But Torbitt lives on. Like all good conspiracy theories, it is immune to refutation.[16]

More 'Lone Assassins'

Garrison's case failed: Shaw was acquitted and died in the process of suing Garrison in 1974. The year following Garrison's investigation saw the public execution of Martin Luther King and Kennedy's younger brother (and his attorney general) Robert. Once again, 'lone assassins' were abroad. King had been moving away from the pursuit of civil rights for black Americans to a multiracial campaign against poverty and inequality and he was a leader of the opposition to the war in Vietnam. Robert Kennedy, also opposed to the Vietnam war, looked set to become the Democratic candidate in the 1968 election. (It is tempting to conclude that the people who killed his brother were getting nervous at the prospect of President Bobby Kennedy. However there is no evidence on this. It is clear that Sirhan didn't shoot Robert but the precise reason for the assassination is unknown.) King and Robert were killed by conspiracies which had learned some lessons from Dallas. King's 'assassin', a minor criminal named James Earl Ray, was more convincingly framed than was Oswald but the 'evidence' wasn't tested. Threatened with the death sentence if found guilty, the veteran con Ray took a plea bargain, pleading guilty in exchange for his life and thus there was no trial.[17] The murder of Robert Kennedy provided not a patsy but a live 'assassin' blazing away at him in a crowded room. This obscured various awkward facts about the event, notably that the autopsy showed unequivocally that Robert Kennedy had been killed by a shot fired at point blank range – a couple of inches or less – behind his ear and that all the shots which hit him had come from his rear. But Sirhan was in front of him.[18] The King shooting looked iffy from the outset and, by

1971, the Sirhan solution to the Robert Kennedy case, absurd though it must have seemed to challenge it at the time, since Sirhan had been seen firing a gun by dozens of people, had been taken apart. The Kennedy researchers knew that the Dallas shooting was just the first of three. Were they linked? Was there a 'power control group', some central body doing the killing?[19]

From Dallas to Watergate and its Aftermath

From 1966 to 1976, as the Vietnam war and the opposition to it radicalised large numbers of Americans, there was a continuous stream of revelations about the role of the US intelligence and security services abroad and in domestic American politics and society. Opposition to the war fuelled a large radical inquiry into the Cold War and part of America's hidden history was revealed. CIA officers began spilling the beans about the CIA for the first time.[20] The military-industrial complex – really the military-industrial-intelligence-media complex – about which retiring President Eisenhower had warned America a decade earlier, began to be critically examined and exposed for the first time.

In the middle of this there was Watergate: the discovery that the techniques of the covert operations of intelligence services – burglaries, buggings, disinformation – were being deployed out of the Nixon White House basement against journalists, ordinary citizens and political opponents. Figures from the CIA's anti-

Castro operations of a decade earlier turned up in the White House 'plumbers' unit caught bugging the Democratic National Committee office in the Watergate office complex. The delirious prospect opened up of the Kennedy assassination being somehow linked to Watergate. Maybe there really was a single 'secret team' working behind the scenes and manipulating America! But Watergate linked the 'plumbers' in the White House basement not to the assassination – of that there was no evidence – but rather to the CIA's operations against Cuba. *Cuba again*.

The Vietnam war also began feeding into the direction of some of the Kennedy assassination researchers. As part of the bureaucratic war over who would carry the can for the failure in Vietnam, a long study of the war, which became known as the Pentagon Papers, was leaked by Daniel Ellsberg.[21] Peter Dale Scott, a Canadian diplomat turned academic, began in the 1960s with an interest in the politics surrounding US involvement in Vietnam and moved from there to an interest in the killing of Kennedy. Scott noticed that some crucial documentation of the political decisions which led to US involvement had been distorted in the Pentagon Papers account. Specifically, one document, NSAM273, which expressed JFK's intention to withdraw from Vietnam, had been omitted, thus creating a false continuity between the Vietnam policies of the Kennedy and Johnson administrations. In 1976, Scott wrote: 'The systematic censorship and distortion of NSAM273, first by the Pentagon Papers and later by the *New York Times*, suggests that the Kennedy assassination was itself an important, perhaps a crucial event, in the history of the Indochina war.'[22]

The torrent of revelations about the secret agencies and covert operations impacted on the Kennedy assassination case in two ways. More people began writing books about the case, incorporating some of the new, post Watergate information. Two of the better ones of this period were Robert Sam Anson's *They've Killed the President: the Search for the Murderers of John F. Kennedy*, and the anthology *The Assassinations: Dallas and Beyond — A Guide to Cover-ups and Investigations.*[23] Both books covered the same material; virtually all the possible culprits — with the exception of LBJ and the KGB — are discussed, though with different emphases. In *The Assassinations*, there is very little on organised crime. The whole thrust of the book is towards the American intelligence services and the idea that Kennedy's murder had something to do with the Vietnam war is prominent.[24] In *The Assassinations* Jack Ruby is a bit player; in Anson's book he gets 28 pages.[25]

The revelations of covert operations by the CIA and FBI began to threaten to spill into the mainstream political area. After Nixon fell, Gerald Ford replaced him as president. Out of the Watergate revelations had come the tricky issue of what the CIA had been doing in America. President Ford, who had been on the Warren Commission, created another 'commission', under

Nelson Rockefeller, to 'investigate' this. Appointed to the Rockefeller 'commission' was the lawyer David Belin who, like Ford, had served on the Warren Commission. Do we detect continuities here? More important were the creation of the Senate Select Committee on Intelligence Affairs (full title: Select Committee to Study Governmental Operations with Respect to Intelligence Activities), chaired by Democrat Frank Church, which became known as the Church Committee and a parallel committee in the House of Representatives, the House Select Committee on Intelligence, known, after its chairman Otis Pike, as the Pike Committee.[26]

While reporting on CIA assassination plots abroad, both the Church Committee and the separate inquiry chaired by Nelson Rockefeller had declined to look at the King and Kennedy assassinations of the previous decade. But two members of the Church Committee, Republican Richard Schweiker and Democrat Gary Hart, were allowed to create a subcommittee *not* to investigate who killed Kennedy but to investigate the performance of the intelligence agencies *in relation to* the Kennedy assassination. They hired one researcher, Gaeton Fonzi, a journalist who had been interested in the case since the 1960s, and Fonzi became the first person employed by the US federal government to investigate the Kennedy assassination who assumed it had been a conspiracy. But the subcommittee had limited time and limited budget and, just when Fonzi found an apparently important lead, the subcommittee was wound up. The chair of the main committee, Frank Church, 'was chomping at the bit, anxious to get into the Presidential sweepstakes', and wanted his committee's report published. The Hart/Schweiker subcommittee was forced to issue a report with what it had.[27]

None of the committees of this period really tried to challenge the American intelligence and security bureaucracies. All were compromises between the perceived popular demand for investigation, the politicians' anxiety at handling 'national security' issues, and the desire of the committees' leading players to use them for personal publicity. In his memoir, *The Last Investigation,* Fonzi comments that Schweiker was 'ecstatic at the press reception of the report' (p. 163), so encouraged that he briefly seemed inclined to continue his Kennedy investigation without the backing of the Church Committee after its demise. Then he was offered the position of vice-presidential candidate on the Ronald Reagan ticket for the 1976 Republican presidential nomination and gave up his interest in the assassination.[28]

Hard to imagine though this now is, looking at the America of the past 27 years, such was the climate generated by the CIA and FBI revelations, Watergate and the war in Vietnam, that the momentum for an investigation into the King and Kennedy killings continued in Congress:

So with the Black Caucus [in Congress] and the Warren Commission critics putting political pressure on the House leadership, bills [initiated in 1975] to investigate both the King and Kennedy assassinations, after being locked in committees for the past year, were finally pushed through. And the House Select Committee on Assassinations was begotten.[29]

The House Select Committee on Assassinations; or The Same River Twice

This committee was no different from those which had preceded it in the previous two years: the political system felt it had to be seen to do something; but not very much. To the naive outsider, such as the author, then just beginning to take an interest in the subject at that time, it might have looked like an investigation into the biggest murder case of American history but, to the politicians, it was just another committee. The Kennedy researchers viewed it with a scepticism which was amply justified. Fonzi and a bunch of young law graduates and policemen, none of whom had any expertise in the case, were hired. Some research was done and a lot of bureau-cratic nonsense and politicking took place. When the first director of research, Richard Sprague, officially staff director and chief counsel, tried to mount a serious investigation and asked for a large staff, a big budget and subpoena powers, he was fired by the committee. Something more modest was required. Sprague had misunderstood the situation. The Kennedy researchers knew then that the game was over. For the committee's research staff it was intensely frustrating: they generated some good new information to find that there was no interest in it:

> There is not one investigator – not one – who served on the Kennedy task force of the Assassinations Committee who honestly feels he took part in an adequate effort, let alone the 'full and complete' investigation mandated by Congress. In fact most of the investigators have bitter memories of the limitations and direction imposed upon them.[30]

As happened with the Warren Commission, the politicians on the committee took little serious interest in it once they had a chief counsel, Robert Blakey, who was politically savvy and knew which doors not to try and open – in this case the CIA's:

> For Congressmen whose priority is political survival – no exception comes to mind here – an investigation into Kennedy's assassination holds absolutely no political profit. It's a no-win game. In fact, most Congressmen see it as a minefield laced with political barbed wire that just might cut a career to shreds.[31]

Blakey knew that his job wasn't to investigate the assassinations but merely to produce a report for his committee by the agreed deadline and he sidelined the various leads generated by the research teams. Blakey had decided that organised crime had done the deed and used the public hearings towards the end of the committee's existence to sell his conclusion about the Mob's responsibility. There was almost a hitch. One of the committee's scientific panels, examining a piece of recording tape of sounds apparently collected by a police motorcycle microphone in the motorcade, concluded that the tape appeared to show that Oswald was not the only shooter and that – maybe – there was a shot from the Grassy Knoll.[32] Unable to get round the acoustic evidence which arrived late in the day, Blakey's report simply fudged it. It concluded that JFK was 'probably assassinated as the result of a conspiracy'; that nonetheless Lee Harvey Oswald fired the fatal shots; and it hinted that the Mob was responsible, though offering no specific evidence to support that view. Quite how apparent left-winger Lee Harvey Oswald fitted into a Mob conspiracy was left unexplained. The *New York Times*, which had supported the Warren Commission's verdict of a lone assassin to the bitter end, drew an appropriately absurd further conclusion. Two shooters? Then there must have been two lone assassins who, coincidentally, turned up at Dealey Plaza on the same day and fired at the same time.[33]

Notes

1. One of my favourite hypotheses about the case is the idea that JFK was killed by the American Mafia, working for their Italian cousins, who were working for the CIA in Italy where the agency had helped keep the Italian right in power since 1948. This can be elaborated quite a way with material on the anxiety aroused within Cold War breasts by Kennedy's tolerance of the Italian Communist Party and the presence of well known Kennedy hater, the CIA's William Harvey, in the US embassy in Rome. But ultimately there is, alas, no evidence for this elegant supposition.

2. Garrison, by then a judge, appears briefly as himself in *The Big Easy*, the 1986 movie set in New Orleans and starring Dennis Quaid.

3. Garrison's case against Shaw is demolished in a series of articles beginning at <http://mcadams.posc.mu.edu/shaw1.htm>. Shaw did a pretty good job of rebutting the case against him in an interview in *Penthouse*, vol. 4, no. 8. He told two conspicuous lies, however. First, he ridiculed the idea that someone as well known as himself would use an alias or *nom de guerre* – Garrison said he was also known as 'Clem Bertrand'. This was disingenuous in the extreme: in the gay world of the period such *noms de guerre* were widely used. Whether or not Shaw was 'Bertrand' remains unclear. Secondly, he

denied knowing David Ferrie but there are photographs of them together at a gay party. But Shaw was hiding the gay subculture, not the assassination conspiracy.

4. Ferrie was later dismissed from the Civil Air Patrol for having nude drinking sessions with the boys. This information and the Oswald/Ferrie picture are on pages 19–21 of Robert J. Groden, *The Search for Lee Harvey Oswald* (London: Bloomsbury, 1995).

5. On Andrews see Jim Garrison, *On the Trail of the Assassins* (Harmondsworth: Penguin, 1988), chapter 6.

6. This footage can be seen in Stone's *JFK*. 40 years later it is still startling. There is now evidence that even the Zapruder film had been doctored. See note 25 of the final chapter.

7. In an article in the American journal *The Wilson Quarterly* of Spring 2001, Max Holland quotes a survey showing that 20 per cent fewer Americans accepted the Warren Commission's verdict on the Dallas shooting after the start of Garrison's inquiry than before it.

8. Although Scheim's selection on pp. 47–50 of the evidence is rather persuasive, I find myself unable to believe this, mainly because Garrison wrote three books about the case (*On the Trail of the Assassins* [1988], the earlier *Heritage of Stone* [1970] and a novel *The Star Spangled Contract* [1976]) and I cannot imagine anyone writing three books as a political

favour. One, maybe, but three?

9. This is discussed in great detail in Peter Dale Scott's *Deep Politics and the Death of JFK* (London: University of California Press, 1993), and *Deep Politics II* (Skokie, Illinois: Green Archive Publications, 1995).

10. Scott, ibid., pp. 70–71.

11. Scott ibid., p. 24.

12. Christopher Andrew and Vasili Mitrokhin, *The Mitrokhin Archive* (London: Allen Lane, 1999), pp. 295–6.

13. The book's genesis is discussed in the memoir of the then editor of *Ramparts* magazine, Warren Hinckle, *If You Have a Lemon, Make Lemonade* (New York: GP Putnam's, 1974). Pages 261–5 are a nice account of a French intelligence officer trying to plant his Kennedy thesis on *Ramparts*, then the leading non-affiliated left-wing magazine in the States. But Hinckle was too smart for him. So the thesis had to be produced in book form, printed in Europe and then imported into the US via Canada. I got a copy via the Northern Ireland Kennedy researcher, the late Harry Irwin.

14. This was discussed most recently in Sally Denton and Roger Morris, *The Money and the Power* (New York: Alfred Knopf, 2001), pp. 296–7.

15. It appeared in a left-wing, French-language, Canadian magazine called *Le Devoir*. I have never seen the original but it was discussed in *Canadian Dimension*, September/October 1967. In Garrison's

defence, it was a different time and the world at large knew very little about intelligence operations and there had been no big exposés of intelligence agencies planting disinformation. Europe was a long way away in those days and checking the veracity of a story like that in a foreign country would have been time-consuming, expensive and slow. In today's world the disinformation would have been posted on the Net and refuted within days.

16. Torbitt was most recently republished, with a commentary, as *NASA, Nazis and JFK: The Torbitt Document and the JFK Assassination* (Kempton, Illinois: Adventures Unlimited Press, 1996). Originally circulated as a typescript with '1970' on it, it reached me in 1977. One of *Lobster's* minor contributions to the Kennedy assassination oeuvre was an essay by Stephen Dorril, published in *Lobster* no 2 in 1983, showing the roots of the Permindex story in Soviet disinformation. But *Lobster* then had a print run of 150 and was an A5 magazine done on an electric typewriter, was a long way from America, and noone noticed the article. Dorril's article has been noticed since and is on the Web at <http://mcadams.posc.mu.edu/lobster.htm>. See also <http://mcadams.posc.mu.edu/fairplay.htm> for a devastating assault on some recent attempts to salvage Garrison.

17. The best account of the King assassination – and its solution – is in William Pepper's *Orders to Kill: The*

Truth Behind the Murder of Martin Luther King, (New York: Carroll and Graf, 1995) and its sequel *An Act of State* (London: Verso, 2003). TV producer John Edginton wrote about his study of the King case in 'Prisoner of Silence' in *The Listener*, 28 September 1989.

James Earl Ray died in prison, aged 70, in 1998. Harold Jackson devoted fourth-fifths of his long obituary in *The Guardian* (24 April 1998) to describing Ray's early life and his racism, briefly mentioned the curious fact that the apparently none-too-bright petty criminal Ray had managed to acquire the identities of four men in Toronto who all looked like him, but omitted any of the subsequent research on the King murder, such as that by John Edginton and William Pepper. Godfrey Hodgson's obituary in *The Independent* (25 April 1998) was much better: Hodgson actually knows something about recent developments in the case. In his generally excellent column in *The Observer* on 26 April 1998, Nick Cohen recycled *Searchlight's* assault on Pepper's book on the King conspiracy at the time of its first appearance, dismissing it because one of the many leads Pepper turned up was a Sid Carthew who, unbeknown to Pepper, was a former British National Party member. Cohen used the syllogism first used by *Searchlight*: Carthew is a fascist, therefore Carthew is not reliable; Pepper quoted Carthew, therefore the book is not reliable. In fact

Carthew's evidence is marginal to the book. Did Cohen read the book?

18. The physical evidence that Sirhan didn't shoot Robert Kennedy is much clearer than the evidence that Oswald didn't shoot John. So why has the Robert Kennedy shooting provoked so little interest? 90 per cent of Dan Moldea's *The Killing of Robert Kennedy* (London: Norton, 1995) lays out the overwhelming evidence that Sirhan wasn't the fatal shooter and identifies the only possible candidate for the shooter role: Thane Cesar, the only person standing behind RFK when he was shot. In the final 10 per cent of his book Moldea tracks this character down. He denies it, of course, and offers to take a polygraph test – which he passes. On the basis of that alone Moldea, absurdly, decides that, despite the evidence, it must have been Sirhan. Never heard of people learning to beat polygraphs, Mr Moldea?

19. 'Power control group' was one of several titles for this hypothesised body in this period. 'The secret team' was another.

20. L. Fletcher Prouty, *The Secret Team* in 1973; Victor Marchetti and John Marks, *The CIA and the Cult of Intelligence* appeared in 1974; Philip Agee's *CIA Diary: Inside the Company* in 1975. Agee and Marchetti had been CIA officers; Prouty had been Air Force liaison with the CIA.

21. This was known as the Pentagon Papers. L. Fletcher Prouty claims in his *The Secret Team* that some of the

report was actually written by the CIA.

22. Scott, Hoch and Stetler (eds) *The Assassinations* (Harmondsworth: Penguin, 1978; originally New York, 1976) p. 365.

23. Anson – New York: Bantam, 1975; *The Assassinations* – see note 22.

24. See Peter Dale Scott's landmark essay 'The Death of Kennedy, Vietnam and Cuba' in *The Assassinations* (see note 22).

25. There were two other interesting books in this period. One was Sid Blumenthal and Harvey Yazijian (eds.) *Government by Gunplay: Assassinations Conspiracy Theories from Dallas to Today* (New York: Signet Books, 1976). Like *The Assassinations* (see note 22) this was an anthology, including essays on the deaths of Robert Kennedy and Martin Luther King, the shooting of Governor George Wallace and the assault on the Black Panthers – all of which were then being considered as part of a spectrum of suppressive activity by the American state. Co-editor Blumenthal turns up in the 1990s as senior adviser to, and spin-doctor for, Bill Clinton, and omitted this book from the author blurb on his memoir of the Clinton years, *The Clinton Wars*. The other significant book was Carl Oglesby's *The Yankee and Cowboy War: Conspiracies from Dallas to Watergate*, (Kansas City: Sheed Andrews and McMeel, 1976). In these books we can see the Kennedy assassination still in the mainstream of radical concerns of the

time. The Blumenthal anthology has a foreword by whistle-blowing CIA officer Philip Agee and Oglesby was a former leader of the 1960s radical group SDS, Students for a Democratic Society.

26. A recent account of the formation and impact of these is in chapter 12 of Rhodri Jeffreys-Jones, *Cloak and Dollar: A History of American Secret Intelligence* (London: Yale University Press, 2002). The complex politics around the formation and activities of the committees is discussed in the introduction by Philip Agee to *CIA: The Pike Report* (Nottingham: Spokesman, 1977). Some of the Church Committee's work can be found at the website containing the details of the FBI's Cointelpro operations, <www.cointel.org>. The Pike Committee's report was published in the UK as *CIA: The Pike Report* (Nottingham: Spokesman, 1977).

    The Rockefeller 'commission' was rubbished in 'The Rockefeller Commission: The Second JFK Whitewash' by Robert and Christine Groden in *Argosy*, October 1977.

27. Gaeton Fonzi, *The Last Investigation* (New York: Thunder's Mouth Press, 1993) p. 146. Chapters 8–17 of Fonzi's memoir describe this period. Fonzi's is one of the essential books in this field.

28. The choice of Schweiker as an ally for the far-right Ronald Reagan always looked odd to me but, as far as I know, none of the Kennedy assassination researchers have pursued the idea that Schweiker

was chosen precisely to put a stop to his interest in JFK's death.

29. Fonzi (see note 27) p. 171. This period of transition from Watergate through the CIA/FBI revelations to the House Select Committee on Assassinations is the subject of the introduction to the anthology *The Assassinations*. See note 22 above.

30. Fonzi (see note 27) p. 402. Fonzi's account of the bureaucratic warfare in and around the committee is fascinating.

31. Fonzi (see note 27) p. 403.

32. How a tape consisting almost entirely of motorcycle engine noise can be treated to show not only shots but where they came from is beyond my ken. And, of course, there are people who dispute this inter-pretation of the police motorbike tape. I know so little about this subsection of the assassination that I don't even know what the status of the tape evidence is now among the researchers. The acoustic evidence is even less accessible to a general reader than the medical evidence – and that's now virtually unintelligible.

33. HSCA findings are at <http://www.geocities.com/jfkinfo/hscareport.htm>.

The House Select Committee
on Assassinations and Beyond

From Cover-up to Conspiracy?

Because there is enough evidence to plausibly construct an initial case for many candidates, the Kennedy assassination has always been a kind of mirror which reflects the researcher's and reader's own preoccupations and prejudices. In the late 1960s and 1970s, as knowledge became available about the US intelligence and security services and their activities, they came to dominate thinking about the assassination. Initially, the main focus of this was Cuba and the CIA's secret war against Castro. Oswald's actions in the years before the assassination could be superficially read as suggesting that he was either a pro- or an anti-Castro activist. But, as the death toll in Vietnam rose and the opposition to the war became fiercer, the Vietnam dimension became more prominent. After the Pentagon Papers, the fact that the US policy on Vietnam was changed within two days of Kennedy's death, and the fact that the change had been concealed, loomed larger.

Peter Dale Scott, who detected this covert policy

shift, had already signalled in his little book on the Schweiker/Hart subcommittee report, discussed in the previous chapter, *Crime and Cover-up: The CIA, the Mafia, and the Dallas-Watergate Connection* (Berkeley, CA: Westworks, 1977), that he was moving away from the whodunnit aspects of the case into what he referred to as parapolitics, 'the dark quadrant... where CIA, private intelligence, and Mafia operations overlap'.[1] Scott is a master, and his work is the most important single source on US politics since the Kennedy assassination. When I met him in 1986, we talked at length about JFK and he said that he didn't think we would ever find out who pulled the trigger – but that wasn't the important thing anyway. As the information on the events expanded, Scott moved further and further into the background of the surface events and his work got more and more dense.[2] Finally he stopped using the term parapolitics and began referring to 'deep politics'.[3]

HSCA and the Mob-Did-It Verdict

Few of the Kennedy researchers accepted the assertions by House Select Committee on Assassins (HSCA) Chief Counsel, Robert Blakey, that the Mob had done it. The verdict felt like a cop-out, a fallback position, a cover story created to conceal the uglier truth of action by the secret state. But the reason Blakey could suggest this scenario in the HSCA report, against the wishes of most of his staff, was that the case for the Mafia as the culprits made immediate sense. The Mob had the means and killing people is something they did routinely. Killing a president is something a bit special, but it is clear from the transcripts of bugged conversations of Mafia personnel that the Mob did not hold the president in awe. He was just Joe Kennedy's son, another shyster politician whom they thought they could control by giving money and political help in the 1960 election. The Mob had the motive: they were being seriously hassled by the Justice Department headed by Robert Kennedy. We know, again from FBI intercepts, that they talked repeatedly of killing both Kennedys.[4] The event itself, the crudity of the method chosen – firing at him in public – and, most of all, the role of Ruby in clearing up the mess, suggest that the Mafia did it.

Many of the assassination researchers have been reluctant to acknowledge the strength of 'the Mafia-did-it' case. Against it the argument is always made that, powerful though they might have been, the Mob did not have the muscle to organise the cover-up which followed the event. This argument, which presumed that the creators of the cover-up would be, or would lead to, the perpetrators of the assassination, has lost much of its power in the last 30 years as we have seen US politicians and intelligence and military bureaucracies routinely cover-up everything, whether they were directly involved or not, from Dallas, through Watergate, through Iran-Contra and the other intelligence scandals of the Reagan-Bush Snr. era. The fact that agency X covered-up after Oswald's arrest tells us they may have had connections to Oswald, or feared that an investigation of Oswald would reveal other operations, but not, alas, that they had a direct connection to the assassination. The investigation of the Dallas cover-up has been enormously informative about the behaviour of the US intelligence and security bureaucracies but it tells us nothing about the conspiracy. For all the wonderful work done by the JFK researchers, all the trails peter out when they reach Dealey Plaza.

The real difficulty for the Mob theory is the role of Oswald and his many intelligence connections. How does he fit into a Mob plot? Just the patsy, as he himself said in the Dallas police station? Perhaps. David Scheim's *Contract on America* (New York: Shapolsky Publishers, 1988) is the major statement of the Mob-did-it thesis and Oswald is only marginally involved in the story.[5] Scheim tries hard to make much of Oswald's uncle, who may have been a minor figure in the Mob's gambling operations, but there isn't much to go on.

Running more or less in parallel to the House Select Committee investigation, British writer Anthony Summers applied a top flight journalist's research to the job, uncovering a great deal of new information, especially about Oswald's activities in New Orleans, and wrote the best single volume on the assassination, *Conspiracy.*[6] Although he did not reach a conclusion, the selection of evidence he made, and his new discoveries, strengthened the case for both an alliance of anti-

Castro Cubans and renegade CIA personnel or for a
Mob hit.

After HSCA

After HSCA the best publicised events in the field were
Edward J. Epstein's *Legend* (London: Hutchinson/
Arrow, 1978) and David Lifton's *Best Evidence* (New
York: Carroll and Graf, 1980). Restating the Warren
Commission's position – Oswald did it alone – Epstein's
Legend got masses of publicity in the major media on
both sides of the Atlantic from writers and reviewers
who knew nothing about the subject. Epstein did make
one change: where the Warren Report had Oswald as a
lone crazy (albeit with a leftist history) Epstein tried to
convince the reader that Oswald was really working for
the KGB. Epstein was funded by the *Reader's Digest* –
which was used by the CIA in the 1950s and 1960s Cold
War to run disinformation[7] – and hired eight (!)
researchers to reinvestigate Oswald. By dint of
excluding everything known about Oswald which
referred to Cuba or the US intelligence services – and
Epstein had already written about this material in a book
on the Garrison inquiry, *Plot and Counterplot*, so the
omission was witting – Epstein restored Oswald to his
cover role, that of the genuine Marxist defector and
added that, somewhere along the line, the KGB got at
him (though he wasn't quite sure when or how). This
was nonsense and manifestly had less to do with the

Kennedy assassination than it did with the renewal of the Cold War then going on in Washington which led, in 1980, to the election of Ronald Reagan as president.[8] *Legend* was dismissed by the Kennedy researchers and is now rarely mentioned, let alone cited.

In his *Best Evidence*, David Lifton went back to the body – the 'best evidence' in the legal mind. Where many of the other researchers had abandoned the actual events on Dealey Plaza as either not interesting or not useful, a worked-out seam, Lifton had been pursuing the medical and forensic evidence. Like others, Lifton had noticed in the 1960s that there was a flat contradiction between the account of Kennedy's wounds given by the doctors who worked on his body at the Parkland Hospital in Dallas and the account of the wounds in the autopsy report. The Parkland doctors all described a big hole in the back of Kennedy's head where his brains had been blown out. Thus there was a shooter from the front; thus a shooter who was not Lee Harvey Oswald. The autopsy described a different wound, higher up, further forward – a wound (just) consistent with a shot from the rear and thus (just) consistent with Lee Harvey Oswald's alleged shooting position behind Kennedy. 'Fix', cried the buffs when they read the autopsy report; of course they rigged the autopsy to fit Oswald.

To Lifton, this didn't make sense: the autopsy room was packed with the most senior military personnel. Could it really be that they were all party to such a fraud? Some buffs saw this as evidence of a massive conspiracy involving the military but this seemed unlikely to Lifton. But, if the surgeons did an honest autopsy and the wounds *were* different from those seen by the doctors in Dallas, Lifton concluded that somebody *changed the wounds* inflicted in Dallas en route to the autopsy conducted near Washington, DC to make them fit Lee Harvey Oswald, lone assassin, firing from behind the president. Lifton set off to find how and where it was done.

Best Evidence is a wonderful read and, if you turn off the critical faculties, he almost persuades you it all makes sense. But can wounds be reconstructed? Can a large gaping hole in the back of the head be repaired to fool autopsy surgeons? And Lifton didn't just ask the reader to accept that the body was altered in an *ad hoc* response to the lone assassin decision taken in Washington – which is implausible enough – he expects the reader to accept that the original conspiracy had this built into it. In other words, the conspiracy was to kill JFK and frame Oswald, and part of the framing of Oswald would be altering the body to match his firing position. And this is just stupid. Such a ridiculous scheme would fall at the first question: after the assassination, how do you guarantee gaining access to the dead president's body to alter it? The Kennedy researcher community didn't take Lifton seriously but the major media, which normally either ignore or rubbish anything critical of the Warren Commission verdict, did, giving his book extensive praise – including a big spread in *Time* – enough in itself to arouse suspicion.

But if Lifton's explanation is unconvincing, the clash between the Parkland doctors and the autopsy remained: the wounds are not the same.[9] It took nearly 20 years for someone to look at the wound problem and come up with another, even more startling, hypothesis: if the wounds *are* different, if *both* the Parkland doctors and the autopsy team told the truth and the body *wasn't* altered, there must have been *two* bodies. To this I return below.

Notes

1. In this wider field Scott co-wrote *The Iran Contra Connection* (Boston: South End Press, 1987) and *Cocaine Politics* (Berkeley, CA: University of California Press, 1991) before returning to the Kennedy assassination with *Deep Politics and the Death of JFK* (Berkeley, CA: University of California Press, 1993) and *Deep Politics 2* (Skokie, Ill.: Green Archive Publications, 1995).

2. His *Crime and Cover-up: The CIA, the Mafia, and the Dallas-Watergate Connection* consisted of 74 pages, almost a third of them taken up with notes. It had a text index but someone constructed and circulated an index of Scott's end notes – the first instance of this I came across.

3. On the distinctions between the two terms, see Scott's introduction to his forthcoming *Deep Politics*

III at <http://history-matters.com/> which includes the following section, introducing a third term, parahistory: 'Parahistory can be partly recovered by the disclosure of previously repressed records. Deep political history must attempt to reconstruct what happened in areas where there are few if any records at all.'

4. The evidence of this is succinctly summarised in Anthony Summers' biography of J. Edgar Hoover, *Official and Confidential* (London: Gollancz, 1993) pp. 325–333.

5. Another version is John H. Davis, *Mafia Kingfish: Carlos Marcello and the Assassination of John F. Kennedy* (New York: New American Library/Signet, 1989).

6. Republished and updated as *Conspiracy* (New York: Paragon House, 1989 and 1991) and *The Kennedy Conspiracy* (London: Warner, 1996 and 1998).

7. See Fred Landis, 'The CIA and the Reader's Digest' in *Covert Action Information Bulletin* 29 (Winter 1988).

8. In his revised account of the actual shooting, in an appendix 'The Sequence of the Shots', Epstein tells us: 'The Warren Commission… concluded that only two shots were fired accurately, the first striking the President in the back of the neck and passing through him to cause two wounds in Governor Connally; and the second shot exploding the President's head and fragmenting. (A third shot missed completely.)' But four lines later, he assures

us that: '…from the path of the bullets delineated in the autopsy photographs and X-rays (and other collateral evidence) it can be concluded that Kennedy and Connally were hit by two separate bullets and that a third bullet then hit Kennedy.' Epstein is trying to avoid having to swallow the absurdity of the so-called 'magic bullet' which hit Kennedy and Connally and emerged undamaged and so commits himself to three shots striking Kennedy and Connally. But what has happened to the bullet which missed and struck the pavement, sending up a fragment which struck a bystander? With the three shots which hit Kennedy and Connally that makes four shots (never mind the less well publicised bullet which struck the presidential limousine) and Epstein has destroyed his own thesis. And, yes, there is material on the shot which hit the limousine. See, for example, <www.jfklancer.com/LimoMarsh.html> which includes a photograph showing bullet damage to it.

9. A nice clear exposition of this is in Robert Groden's *The Killing of a President* (Harmondsworth: Penguin, 1993) pp. 73–89) which lays out the wound problem, rejects Lifton's thesis but doesn't offer one of its own. Groden's big book illustrates the best and worst of photoanalysis: it is full of wonderful pictures of the event but also contains a lot of blurred images which do not show what Groden claims they do.

In 2006 Douglas Horne, formerly Chief Analyst for Military Records, of the Assassination Records Review Board (ARRB), gave a press conference (which barely anyone attended) and said, *inter alia*: 'I have been studying these records for 10 years now. The reason I am here today is because contained within our deposition transcripts and interview reports is unequivocal evidence that there was a US government cover-up of the medical evidence in the Kennedy assassination, yet most members of the public know nothing about this.' The full text of Horne's statement is at <http://www.jfkresearch.com/forum/index.php?act=ST&f=5&t=5594>.

The problem with the wounds is immediately visible if you use Google Images. Search for 'JFK autopsy' and you will see photographs showing (a) the back of JFK's head clotted with blood and brains and (b) the back of JFK's head undamaged, pristine. Both cannot be true. It really is as simple as that.

True Confessions

One of the odd features of the case is the number of people who have confessed to involvement in the assassination. In 1975, as Kennedy assassination research began to be affected by the Watergate story, about which enquiries had begun in Congress, a woman called Marita Lorenz, sometime lover of Fidel Castro, began a long series of claims to have been part of a group – including Watergate 'plumber' Howard Hunt – which went to Dallas in November 1963 and which, she implied but never quite stated, shot Kennedy. It is clear from the timing of her story and inconsistencies in it that this was disinformation aimed at muddying the water, probably on behalf of the CIA.[1] In 1976, Robert Morrow published *Betrayed,* in which he claimed a peripheral role in the assassination, a claim he renewed in his *First Hand Knowledge: How I Participated in the CIA-Mafia Murder of JFK* (New York: SPI Books, 1992). Morrow's books are full of errors and inconsistencies and his claims have never been taken seriously.[2]

Two people have confessed to being one of the 'tramps' who were photographed being arrested just after the shooting. The official story was that they were a trio of hoboes who were picked up in some railway wagons behind the grassy knoll, taken in by the police for questioning and released. When the photographs of the tramps were published someone noticed that while two of them looked like they might be tramps, the third was wearing rather a good jacket and decent shoes and looked rather untramp-like. Somebody suggested the jacket looked European and he was nicknamed from then on in assassination legend as 'Frenchie'. Various people have been proposed as being 'the three tramps', the most famous of such identifications being that made by AJ Weberman and Michael Canfield in their book *Coup d'Etat in America* (New York: Third Press, 1975).[3] They suggested that the oldest of the three 'tramps' was actually Watergate 'plumber', former CIA officer E. Howard Hunt; and, indeed, there was a resemblance. Canfield and Weberman's enthusiasm for Hunt as a 'tramp' may have had something to do with Hunt's prominence in the Watergate story just before they wrote their book.[4]

This being an age obsessed with celebrity, after Oliver Stone's film *JFK* put the subject back on the front page, people began claiming to have been one of the assassins. Charles Harrelson, father of TV and film star Woody, claimed to be one of the 'tramps'. He looks quite like one of the tramps – the big one – in one photograph. Since he was in prison at the time of his 'confession', on a charge of murdering a judge, his 'confession' was presumed to be a plea bargain gambit, was not taken seriously by legal officials and Harrelson duly retracted it.

More recently one of the tramps was confidently identified as being the late Chauncey Holt, a criminal and counterfeiter. Holt apparently confessed that he had made, and taken to Dallas, sets of fake Secret Service credentials. Eyewitnesses on Dealey Plaza met a man displaying 'Secret Service' credentials just after the shooting in places where there were no official Secret Service personnel. Holt's daughter had a website for a while, putting forward this story, advocating her daddy's part in the crime of the century.[5] Adding to the muddle, Holt told one researcher that he was at Dealey Plaza with … Charles Harrelson.[6]

But at the web address <http://mcadams.posc.mu.edu/3tramps.htm> the entire 'tramps' puzzle dissolves. The police arrest records of the three 'tramps' were finally released and two of the 'tramps' were tracked down (one was dead) and admitted to being – yes – hoboes at the time. The sister of the dead one cheerfully acknowledged that her brother was a hobo and a drinker who rode the freight trains. It was exactly as the police said it was. All three had been given a bath, haircut and a bed at a hostel in Dallas the night before they were photographed. Next morning they were kitted out with second-hand clothes. 'Frenchie's' 'European' jacket and shoes had come from a charity shop (what the Americans call thrift stores).

Another man in prison, James Files, confessed in 1994 to being one of the assassins. Claiming to be ex-US military and an associate of a mafia leader named Charles Nicoletti, he said he and Nicoletti were involved, and that Nicoletti had done the shooting from the Grassy Knoll.[7] Conveniently for Files, Nicoletti died in the 1970s and, despite the impressive website advocating his claims, there is no obvious reason to believe any of Files' story. To date, noone of substance in the JFK conspiracy world has taken up his cause.

Another candidate as the shooter on the grassy knoll was the late Roscoe White. His son and late wife put him forward for the role and produced documents apparently demonstrating this. Initially this looked plausible, as White had been in the Dallas police force at the time of the shooting and had been in the Marines at the same time as Oswald. But on closer inspection it proved specious.[8] A man called T. Casey Brennan has 'confessed' to all manner of people – including this writer – that he shot JFK while under mind control.[9]

'Mac' Wallace

In 1971, Mark Collom contacted hepatitis and was put in an isolation ward in a hospital. Also there was another hepatitis carrier, a Native American named Loy Factor, by Collom's account a childlike figure of limited intelligence, brain-damaged during military service in WW2. Factor was serving a 44-year sentence for a murder he claimed he didn't do. Collom and Factor spent several months together, and eventually Factor told Collom that he had been involved in the Kennedy assassination. Four years later Collom met up with an old school-friend, Glen Sample, and told him of the encounter with Factor in hospital. Eventually they taped what they knew and sent it to a journalist connection of Sample's. But nothing happened and they concluded that it had been a dead end. In 1992, however, with the Kennedy assassination on the front page thanks to Oliver Stone, Collom contacted Larry Howard who was then director of the JFK Assassination Information Centre in Dallas and told him the Factor story. Howard did some preliminary research into Factor and discovered that some of Factor's story checked out. This encouraged Sample and Collom to track Factor down and revisit the strange tale he had told Collom over a decade before.

In 1994, Glen Sample put out a press release claiming that Factor, by then deceased, had confessed before he died that he was involved in the assassination. Nobody took much notice. A year later he and Mark Collom put out a self-published book on the subject, *The Men on the Sixth Floor* (Garden Grove, CA: Sample Graphics, 1995) about Loy Factor's story and their attempts to stand it up. Nobody took much notice of that, either.[10] That the book got ignored isn't terribly surprising. In the wake of Stone's *JFK* there was a torrent of books about the subject; theirs was self-published; they obviously didn't know much about the subject; it was based on another 'confession' and by this time there had been a number of such 'confessions' to which JFK researchers had devoted some time and energy, all of which had proved to be bogus. Most damaging of all, Factor's story contained what appeared to be absurd elements, notably the claim that Lee Harvey Oswald had been involved in the shooting. But an event three years later changed things and Factor's strange story began to look less ridiculous. The book Sample and Collom wrote and published is an account of interviewing the old and ailing Factor and then trying to check out his story. This is a summary of that story.

Factor met a man he knew only as Wallace in 1962 at the funeral of a Texas politician. Factor said he went along just to see some famous people. In the course of their conversation, Factor boasted to Wallace of his shooting and hunting skills. Wallace was interested and asked for Factor's address. A year later he turned up and asked for a demonstration of Factor's shooting ability. Having seen it, the man told Factor that he might have a job for him in the future using his rifle, a job worth $10,000 – $2,000 immediately and the rest when the job was done. Factor accepted the $2,000. He knew that that job would involve shooting somebody. To a poor Native American, living in the backwoods, this was a lot of money. Later the man sent for Factor to do the job. Factor was taken to a house in Dallas where he met Jack Ruby, the man called Wallace, Lee Harvey Oswald and a young Hispanic woman, Ruth Ann. They ended up on the sixth floor of the book depository.

> At the approach of the motorcade rounding Elm street, Ruth Ann counted down the signal – 'One . . . two . . . three' – while at the same time waving her hand downward on each number. On the down stroke of three the gunmen fired a single shot each, then fled quickly down the stairs – Ruth Ann and Factor to their parked car, Oswald and Wallace in different directions. Loy was driven to the bus depot, a few blocks away where he was to catch a bus back home. But in a short while Ruth Ann and Wallace both returned to the depot to pick up Factor and drive him out of town.[11]

Few of the students of the assassination read this book when it first came out, and those who did dismissed it. For it is almost universally believed by them that, whatever else he did that day, Oswald didn't fire a rifle. In any case, Oswald's movements after the shooting are known. He didn't flee down the back stairs and go off with the assassination gang. He was drinking a Coke in the book depository canteen where he was confronted by one of the policemen who entered the building after the shooting. In this central detail Factor's story is, apparently, simply false and it says something about Sample and Collom's lack of knowledge of the case at the time that they didn't appear to know this.

However, absurd or not, the striking thing about this Loy Factor 'confession' *now* is the reference in 1994 –

and originally in the 1971 conversation with Mark Collom – to the presence of the man called Wallace in Factor's story. For four years *after* the Sample press release about Loy Factor, a fingerprint of one Malcolm 'Mac' Wallace was positively matched with that of an unidentified fingerprint found on a cardboard box in 'the sniper's nest' on the sixth floor of the Texas Book Depository that day in 1963.[12] As cardboard does not apparently retain fingerprints for long, it is virtually certain that Malcolm 'Mac' Wallace left his fingerprint on 'Box A' on the sixth floor of the Texas School Book Depository on the morning of 22 November 1963.[13]

Factor's account of the mechanics of the shooting is unsatisfactory at best. He claims that, while he was on the sixth floor of the book depository and in possession of a rifle, he didn't actually fire at JFK. This is hard to credit. But if this is not credible, why should we believe his story about Ruby and Oswald being part of the plot? The only reason that anyone took his story seriously at all is his identification of 'Wallace' as being in the plot and, in particular, the fact that, from photographs shown him by Collom and Sample, he had identified the 'Wallace' in his account as being 'Mac' Wallace *before* the identification of Wallace's print in the 'sniper's nest'.

The identification of his fingerprint at 'the sniper's nest' was made public in May 1998 when Walt Brown, author of four books on the assassination, representing a 'group of Texas researchers', called a press conference in Dallas to announce that the single hitherto unidentified print had been identified as that of Malcolm 'Mac' Wallace – the man at the centre of the Sample and Collom account of the assassination.[14] As physical evidence goes, this is the biggest event in the case since 1963 and it is astounding that this story didn't get much attention from the major media. But who is 'Mac' Wallace?

'Mac' Wallace and LBJ

On the day before the assassination, Vice President Lyndon Baines Johnson's political future was bleak. He was going to be dumped by the Kennedys as the vice presidential candidate in the 1964 election and there was a pretty good chance he was going to end up in jail. Robert Caro's wonderful account of Johnson's early political career[15] shows that Johnson was a wholly corrupt man: a man who fixed the first election – at college – in which he ever took part, a man who openly stole the election in the 1948 Senate race and a man who became a major fixer and bagman in Congress and the Senate.[16] There was nothing subtle or concealed about this. By the late 1950s, after a career as a poorly paid, public official, Johnson had become a multimillionaire, with large property-holdings in Texas, including a radio station. (A more charitable view would say that Caro's books show a master politician playing the game the way the game was played and trying to do right by his constituents – certainly in the early years.)

By 1962, LBJ's empire of of influence was threatening to come apart. Two major political scandals in which he was involved were slowly being dragged into the light. One involved a Texas conman called Billy Sol Estes who was running a vast scam getting federal agricultural subsidies – $21 million a year, according to Estes, which would approximate to, what, $500 million in today's money? – for 'growing' and 'storing' non-existent crops of cotton and fertiliser. Estes had been paying off Texas politicians since the 1950s. A Department of Agriculture official named Henry Marshall began investigating the Estes racket and was murdered in June 1961. The local Justice of the Peace, 'a Johnson crony' in one contemporary account, who conducted the post-mortem, found that Marshall had committed suicide... by shooting himself five times with a bolt-action rifle.

Others in the Billy Sol Estes story died after Marshall. George Krutilnek, an accountant who worked for Estes, Harold Orr, a businessman involved with Estes, and Howard Pratt, who worked for another Estes company, all apparently died of carbon monoxide poisoning from car engines.[17] J. Evetts Haley, from whose account I am taking this, has a dry footnote at his reference to the second of the carbon monoxide victims which reads: 'The high incidence of carbon monoxide mortality is the subject of an article by Clyde Walters, *Amarillo-Globe-Times*, March 26, 1964.' Death by carbon monoxide poisoning in a car became known as 'a Texas suicide'. A Senate inquiry into Estes slowly got underway but

Johnson's supporters slowed the inquiry down. Estes kept his mouth shut and Johnson, when he became president, got the inquiry shut down. Estes was eventually convicted of fraud in 1968 but never spoke of Johnson.

The other burgeoning scandal in 1963 centred round an LBJ protégé in the Senate named Bobby Baker. Though formally a minor Senate official, Baker was part of LBJ's influence network. Baker opened a motel and club at which he provided booze and sex for Washington's politicians. (Looking back on it, there is a sense that the network of graft which was Washington politics was all getting just a bit blatant.) In 1963 some of Baker's activities were exposed and the Senate Rules Committee began an investigation. There is a much quoted section in the memoir of a Washington lobbyist of the period, Robert Winter-Berger, in which he describes how, a few months after Johnson became president, he was in the office of John McCormack, the Speaker of the House, when LBJ walked in and began discussing the ongoing Bobby Baker problem:

> John, that son-of-a-bitch is going to ruin me. If that cocksucker talks I'm gonna land in jail... I practically raised that motherfucker and now he's gonna make me the first President of the United States to spend the last days of his life behind bars.[18]

The whole of chapter two of Winter-Berger's memoir, 'McCormack's Parlour', is worth reading as a short introduction to the reality of American politics. Most interesting of all, it contains an account of the efforts made by the major media to ignore the Baker story and the attempts by *both* political parties to suppress the inquiry. Winter-Berger notes on pp. 57/8:

> Legislation specifically giving Bobby Baker tax breaks on some of his personal business ventures had been passed in both Houses, passed by members who were willing to do a favor for the bright young man who had been Lyndon Johnson's protégé for so many years... Because Washington DC is a company town, engaged in the business of politics, such a scandal within the federal structure and concerning someone with the highest connections caused a complete panic.

Legislation to cut the taxes of a junior Senate employee? In the event Baker stayed *shtum*, took the rap and emerged from prison to write a bland memoir in which he denied almost everything.[19]

J. Evetts Haley's 1964 version of the Billy Sol Estes events, including the deaths around the Estes scandal, begins with an account of the 1951 murder of John Kinser who, at that time, was dating LBJ's sister, Josefa. Kinser was murdered by Malcolm 'Mac' Wallace at the pitch and putt course owned by Kinser. Wallace was convicted of first degree murder and sentenced in 1952 to... a five year suspended sentence! 'Mac' Wallace, Evetts Haley tells us, had gone to Washington after graduation and worked for Lyndon Johnson before being attached to the Department of Agriculture as an 'economist'.[20] Haley implies that Wallace was working for Lyndon when he killed John Kinser. Juxtaposing the Kinser murder and the deaths surrounding Billy Sol Estes, Haley was telling the reader, without actually saying it, that Wallace had something to do with those deaths.

'Mac' Wallace died in a car crash in 1971 but he was not forgotten. After Billy Sol Estes came out of prison, he testified before a grand jury which had reopened the case of the 'suicide' of Henry Marshall:

> A Texas Ranger, Clint Peoples, had befriended Estes and convinced him that he should come clean with the whole truth. True to his word, Estes agreed to appear before a Robertson County grand jury and clear the record concerning the cotton allotments, the death of Henry Marshall and the involvement of LBJ and others. He recounted the whole ugly picture – from the millions he had funnelled into Johnson's secret slush fund, to the illegal cotton allotment scheme, to the murder of Henry Marshall. Estes testified that Lyndon Johnson, Cliff Carter [an aide of LBJ], Malcolm Wallace and himself met several times to discuss the issue of the 'loose cannon' – Henry Marshall. Marshall had refused an LBJ-arranged promotion to Washington headquarters, and it was feared that he was about to talk. Johnson, according to Estes, finally said, 'Get rid of him', and Malcolm 'Mac' Wallace was given the assignment. According to testimony, Wallace followed Marshall to a remote area of his farm and beat him nearly unconscious. Then, while trying to asphyxiate him with

exhaust from Marshall's pickup truck, Wallace thought he
heard someone approaching the scene, and hastily grabbed
a rifle which customarily rested in the window rack of the
truck. Quickly pumping five shots into Marshall's body,
Wallace fled the scene.[21]

The 1984 grand jury changed the verdict on the death of
Henry Marshall from suicide to death by gunshot.

News of these events in Texas reached Washington and
Estes was contacted by the Justice Department. There
followed an exchange of letters between Estes' lawyer
and a member of the Justice Department. In the letter
from Estes' lawyer, Douglas Caddy, the following
section appeared:

August 9, 1984

Mr. Stephen S. Trott
Assistant Attorney General, Criminal Division
U.S. Department of Justice
Washington, D. C. 20530
RE: Mr. Billie Sol Estes

Dear Mr. Trott:

My client, Mr. Estes, has authorized me to make this
reply to your letter of May 29, 1984. Mr. Estes was a
member of a four-member group, headed by Lyndon
Johnson, which committed criminal acts in Texas in the

1960's. The other two, besides Mr. Estes and LBJ, were Cliff Carter and Mac Wallace. Mr. Estes is willing to disclose his knowledge concerning the following criminal offenses:

I. Murders
1. The killing of Henry Marshall
2. The killing of George Krutilek
3. The killing of Ike Rogers and his secretary
4. The killing of Harold Orr
5. The killing of Coleman Wade
6. The killing of Josefa Johnson
7. The killing of John Kinser
8. The killing of President J. F. Kennedy.

Mr. Estes is willing to testify that LBJ ordered these killings, and that he transmitted his orders through Cliff Carter to Mac Wallace, who executed the murders. In the cases of murders nos. 1–7, Mr. Estes' knowledge of the precise details concerning the way the murders were executed stems from conversations he had shortly after each event with Cliff Carter and Mac Wallace.

In addition, a short time after Mr. Estes was released from prison in 1971, he met with Cliff Carter and they reminisced about what had occurred in the past, including the murders. During their conversation, Carter orally compiled a list of 17 murders which had been committed, some of which Mr. Estes was unfamiliar with. A living witness was present at that meeting and should be willing to testify about it. He is Kyle Brown, recently of Houston and now living in Brady, Texas.

Mr. Estes, states that Mac Wallace, whom he describes as a 'stone killer' with a communist background, recruited Jack Ruby, who in turn recruited Lee Harvey Oswald. Mr. Estes says that Cliff Carter told him that Mac Wallace fired a shot from the grassy knoll in Dallas, which hit JFK from the front during the assassination.

Mr. Estes declares that Cliff Carter told him the day Kennedy was killed, Fidel Castro also was supposed to be assassinated and that Robert Kennedy, awaiting word of Castro's death, instead received news of his brother's killing.

Mr. Estes says that the Mafia did not participate in the Kennedy assassination but that its participation was discussed prior to the event, but rejected by LBJ, who believed if the Mafia were involved, he would never be out from under its blackmail.

Mr. Estes asserts that Mr. Ronnie Clark, of Wichita, Kansas, has attempted on several occasions to engage him in conversation. Mr. Clark, who is a frequent visitor to Las Vegas, has indicated in these conversations a detailed knowledge corresponding to Mr. Estes' knowledge of the JFK assassination. Mr. Clark claims to have met with Mr. Jack Ruby a few days prior to the assassination, at which time Kennedy's planned murder was discussed.

Mr. Estes declares that discussions were had with

Jimmy Hoffa concerning having his aide, Larry Cabell, kill Robert Kennedy while the latter drove around in his convertible.

Mr. Estes has records of his phone calls during the relevant years to key persons mentioned in the foregoing account...'[22]

In his letter Caddy asked for a number of assurances of immunity for his client, Estes. Such assurances the Justice Department were unwilling to give, and nothing came of the contact.[23]

The Estes allegations are fascinating but there are obvious difficulties with them. A convicted conman and fraudster is almost the personification of an unreliable witness and, although he claimed in a 1999 interview with a French magazine that he has evidence in the shape of recorded phone calls with LBJ and Cliff Carter, these have not been made public. Further, Estes' story is an expansion and elaboration of the story in the 1964 Haley book, which, while largely unknown outside the US, sold tens of thousands of copies there. Estes must have been aware of its existence.[24] Of the eight murders he lists, four appeared in the 1964 Haley book, with a strong hint that Wallace was the killer. The possibility exists that Estes simply adopted the existing story and elaborated it. The letter from Estes' lawyer in itself is not evidence of anything; the letter contains interesting allegations, no more.

However, the Estes allegations were made *before* the

identification of 'Mac' Wallace's fingerprint in 'the sniper's nest' and seven years *before* Loy Factor first identified Wallace, from photographs shown him by Sample and Collom, as being the Wallace he was talking about.

And there is more.

In her memoir *Mornings in Texas*, LBJ's mistress, the late Madeleine Brown, wrote the following:

> On Thursday night, Nov. 21, 1963, the last evening prior to Camelot's demise, I attended a social at Clint Murchison's home. It was my understanding that the event was scheduled as a tribute honoring his long time friend, J. Edgar Hoover (whom Murchison had first met decades earlier through President William Howard Taft), and his companion, Clyde Tolson. Val Imm, the society editor for the now-defunct *Dallas Times Herald*, unwittingly documented one of the most significant gatherings in American history. The impressive guest list included John McCloy, Richard Nixon, George Brown, R. L. Thornton, H. L. Hunt and a host of others from the 8F group. The jovial party was just breaking up when Lyndon made an unscheduled visit. I was the most surprised by his appearance since Jesse had not mentioned anything about Lyndon's coming to Clint's. With Lyndon's hectic schedule, I never dreamed he could attend the big party. After all, he had arrived in Dallas on Tuesday to attend the Pepsi-Cola convention. [As had Richard Nixon.] Tension filled the room upon his arrival. The group immediately went behind closed doors. A short time later Lyndon, anxious and red-faced, reappeared. I knew how secretly Lyndon operated. Therefore I said nothing... not even that

I was happy to see him. Squeezing my hand so hard, it felt crushed from the pressure, he spoke with a grating whisper, a quiet growl, into my ear, not a love message, but one I'll always remember: 'After tomorrow those goddamn Kennedys will never embarrass me again – that's no threat – that's a promise.'

The next morning (22 November 1963) Madeleine Brown describes another brief discussion that she had with Lyndon:

I had barely eked out the words, 'About last night…' when his rage virtually went ballistic. His snarling voice jolted me as never before – 'That son-of-a-b—— crazy Yarborough and that g- — - — - – f — - – ing Irish mafia bastard Kennedy will never embarrass me again!' [25]

Is she suggesting that this gathering of politicians and businessmen in some way approved the assassination? Had gathered in Dallas to do so? We cannot ask her: she died in June 2002. In any case, what she claimed happened cannot be true or, at any rate, did not occur on the date she gave. Well known JFK researcher, Gary Mack, found out that LBJ was not there on the evening in question: he was seen and photographed at an event in Houston; and Nixon was elsewhere, seen by two journalists. [26]

Whatever the truth of her party story, it was Madeleine Brown who supplied Sample and Collom with the first name for the 'Wallace' they were given by

Loy Factor. She immediately identified him as Malcolm Wallace, explained the John Kinser murder in 1951 for which Wallace had been convicted, and told them that Wallace had killed Henry Marshall. She added:

> I've said all along that the other shooter in Dealey Plaza that day when Kennedy was killed was none other than Malcolm Wallace. I told Larry [Howard] that the first time I talked to him.[27]

She showed Collom and Sample page 90 of her then unpublished manuscript. She had written:

> Malcolm E. Wallace… who left a trail of bloody murders. To many of us he is still the prime suspect in President Kennedy's assassination. I had met with U.S. Marshall Clint Peoples to discuss Malcolm Wallace because I had witnessed Mac practising at the Dallas Gun Club. He [Peoples] was planning to break the case open with proof that Wallace was one of the shooters behind the picket fence overlooking Dealey Plaza. Unfortunately Clint's untimely death in mysterious circumstances prevented this announcement ever being made…[28]

Three further pieces of evidence have since appeared. The first was the text of a couple of letters which Jack Ruby had smuggled out of his prison in which he points at LBJ, telling whoever was to read the letters that they should read the J. Evetts Haley book which I have quoted above. In one of them he wrote:

…they found some very clever means and ways to trick me and which will be used later as evidence to show the American people that I was part of the conspiracy in the assassination of the president, and I was used to silence Oswald… they alone planned the killing, by they I mean Johnson and others… read the book Texas Looks at Lyndon [sic: a reference to Haley's book *A Texan Looks At Lyndon*] and you may learn quite a bit about Johnson and how he has fooled everyone… In all the history of the US never has a president been elected that has the background of Johnson. Believe me, compared to him I am a Saint.'[29]

The second was a book called *Blood Money and Power* by Barr McClellan (New York: Hanover House, 2003). The book is subtitled 'How LBJ killed JFK' and in it McClellan describes being a lawyer in the Texas law firm headed by Ed Clark, which represented LBJ's interests for many years, and which, on McClellan's account, was the core of Johnson's political machine, bribing (and receiving bribes) and fixing things for LBJ. (Clark was appointed ambassador to Australia by LBJ.) McClellan says that LBJ gave the job of organising the assassination to Clark who, in turn, used Wallace. On close examination, however, McClellan has no direct evidence for any of this. All he has is some circumstantial evidence and the claim that Clark did this made by another partner in the law firm. Worse, woven through McClellan's quite interesting account of the so-called 'bubba justice' system in Texas – what we would probably call the old boy network, i.e. a system based on corruption and violence, run by a tiny minority for their own benefit – are fictional accounts of what he thinks happened that day in Dallas. However, McClellan claims to have known 'Mac' Wallace and seen him around the Clark offices.

The third item is the purported confession of the dying E. Howard Hunt, former CIA officer and one of the Nixon White House's private spies, the 'plumbers'. One of Hunt's sons claims that Hunt confessed to him that he knew who had organised the assassination: a group of senior CIA officers – and LBJ.[30] As yet, the son has not produced the document Hunt is said to have written on his deathbed and we only have the son's word for this.

Neither the McClellan book nor the Hunt 'confession' is substantial but, at the minimum, the two together do show that the LBJ-dunnit thesis is starting to leak into what we might call mainstream JFK research.

The bigger the case, the stronger the proof required. If we don't have a smoking gun with LBJ's prints on it and, if we ignore Madeleine Brown's comments (striking though they are), the Factor confession, the Estes affidavit and the Wallace fingerprint identification are closer to proof than anything which has been discovered before.[31] LBJ had Kennedy killed to save his political career and stay out of jail. It was just more of the same for LBJ and his little group. Texas was a rough old place in 1963 and LBJ was, in effect, running his own crime syndicate.

And he became president.

There is one final striking bit of information in the Sample/Collum book. One of the pieces of the puzzle is the man-who-wasn't-Oswald who went to the Soviet embassy in Mexico City, was photographed outside it by the CIA and identified by the agency at the time as 'Lee Harvey Oswald'. The CIA had the Soviet Embassy wired, heard the man telling the Soviets that he was Lee Harvey Oswald and photographed him on the way out. These photographs are in many of the books on the assassination and the man in the pictures has never been identified.[32] Sample and Collom were contacted by a man called Gene Noblitt who told them that he recognised the man in those photographs: he was a man called Ralph Geb with whom Noblitt had been at school in Texas in the 1930s. Sample and Gollum published pictures of Geb as a young man and there is a resemblance – no more – to the man in the 1963 Mexico City pictures taken 25 years after the Geb pictures. So far, so not very much. But there is a kicker. Who was Ralph Geb's best friend at school? Malcolm 'Mac' Wallace. Was Geb recruited by Wallace as part of the operation to portray Oswald as a Soviet sympathiser?

Considering the tens of millions of hours, the thousand books written, the immense effort by hundreds of people, it is somehow terribly apt that Collom and Sample, starting with no knowledge of the assassination, took the accidentally acquired 1971 confession of a brain-damaged Native American, and solved the case. As soon as Madeleine Brown gave them Wallace's first name, the rest was sitting there in books and newspapers. They didn't have the fingerprint identification of Wallace or the Estes affidavit, which came after the first edition of their book, but they had a lot of it. And it had been sitting there in Texas, while the assassination researchers looked almost everywhere else. Johnson hadn't been considered as a candidate since Joachim Joesten's *The Dark Side of Lyndon Johnson* back in 1968.[33]

Quite how LBJ slipped from the researchers' gaze isn't clear. Partly it was that, from Garrison onwards in 1968, the US state had become the primary focus of the researchers. (Who else had the power to organise the cover-up, was the central question.) Partly it was that when LBJ resigned in 1967 he just got pushed off a crowded agenda: the deaths of King and the second Kennedy, the Watts riots, the Black Panthers, drugs, the Weathermen bombings, Vietnam, the CIA, Watergate, etc etc... Partly it was that, despite the disastrous Vietnam policy, LBJ became thought of as a decent Democrat who pushed through important social legislation – the so-called Great Society programme – on race relations and poverty. And partly it is a tribute to the cover-up organised by LBJ and FBI chief J. Edgar Hoover, the scale of which has only become clear in the last few years.

Notes

1. On Lorenz see Gaeton Fonzi, *The Last Investigation* (New York: Thunder's Mouth Press, 1993), chapter

10. Her claims surfaced in the UK in 'JFK story gains a Mata Hari' in *The Sunday Times*, 6 November 1977.

2. At <http://mcadams.posc.mu.edu/morrow.htm> dozens of errors and inconsistencies in his 1992 book are detailed. Morrow's books coincided with the House Select Committee on Assassinations and Oliver Stone's *JFK*. One of the features of the case is the way disinformation about it appeared whenever there was any kind of investigative action on it.

3. Yes, the same Weberman who, in an earlier incarnation, had become famous as a 'Dylanologist', collecting and analysing Bob Dylan's domestic refuse. From there to a JFK assassination researcher is perhaps not such a big step: both are activities demanding a degree of obsession.

4. The Weberman/Canfield book is a vivid illustration of the desire on the part of many American conspiracy theorists to link everything up together in what Tony Frewin called a unified field theory of conspiracy. This drive to unification is visible all the way through the 1970s and 1980s and reached some kind of peak in the Christic Institute's 1987 account, in *The Affidavit of Daniel P. Sheehan*, of a 'secret team' of CIA personnel responsible for much of the dirty work from Dallas to Iran-Contra. Daniel Sheehan turned up more recently claiming to have been allowed into the National Archives to view government evidence of UFOs crash-landing

on earth. His story is implausible in the extreme. I presented his account and commented on it in *Lobster* 42. Mr Sheehan appears to have been the vehicle for government attempts to spread disinformation about UFOs, of which there have been several. His account is at <http://www.ufomind.com/ufo/updates/2001/jul/m16–015.shtml>. Howard Hunt sued over the allegation that he was part of the Kennedy conspiracy – and eventually lost. He couldn't prove where he had been on 22 November 1963. Could any of us? I remember where I was but have no idea where the people I was with are or if they would remember me. On the Hunt court cases see Mark Lane, *Plausible Denial* (London: Plexus, 1991).

5. Holt's widow and daughter presented their belief that he was 'a tramp' at a big JFK assassination conference in Dallas, 2000. See <http://www.jfklancer.com/Dallas 00.html>. For a while in 2001 his daughter had a website arguing this but it seems to have gone.

6. James Fetzer (ed.) *Assassination Science* (Chicago: Catfeet Press, 1998) p. 368.

7. See <http://www.jfkmurdersolved.com/confession2.htm> and <http://homes.acmecity.com/music/keyboards/688/frept97.htm>.

8. See <http://www.flash.net/~dperry2/roscoew.html> for a very long and impressive account by David Perry of checking out the details of the White

story. This article conveys very clearly the immense labour involved in assessing claims such as these.

9. Here's an extract from Brennan's story:

'Because when I was thirteen, I was being prepared for the blood. I had started school in 1953 in the first grade at five, so, in 1961, I entered Peck High School, in Sanilac County, later to become infamous as the alleged origin of the Oklahoma City bombing plot. At 13, I had already become enamored by the pamphlets provided me, sometimes in huge stacks, by my school board official parents' right-wing political friends. These ranged from the rabble rousing populism of Myron Fagan and the Cinema Educational Guild to the scholarly essays of Dr. Fred G. Schwartz of the Christian Anti-Communism Crusade, which shared offices with the Fair Play for Cuba Committee in New Orleans. Later, in my senior year, Peck teacher Robert Losie would teach a class called 'Communism', based on the Christian Anti-Communist Crusade textbook, YOU CAN TRUST THE COMMUNISTS – TO BE COMMUNISTS by Fred G. Schwartz. At 13, it was eight years since, drugged and terrified, I had first met David Ferrie; two years since I had been taken before the hypnotist J. H. Earnshaw, D.O.; and another two years before those men would kidnap me from the Yale, Michigan airport on November 22, 1963, and force me to fire from the sixth floor storage room of the Texas School

Book Depository Building in Dallas...' <http://pweb.netcom.com/~mthorn/ 3brennan.htm>.

Mr Brennan e-mailed me his story years ago and was terribly disappointed I didn't rush it into print.

10. *Lobster's* reviewer of JFK books, Anthony Frewin, who has read a large proportion of the literature on the case, wrote of it when it appeared: 'Loy Factor? Crazy name, crazy guy. He's a Chickasaw Indian who claims to have been on the sixth floor of the TSBD "helping out" the assassins when JFK was hit. And who was behind the murder? Step forward LBJ. Collom and Sample take Factor at face value and attempt to bolster his claims. Belongs on the shelf next to Henry Hurt's championing of Easterling and the Robert Morrow "confession".'

A new edition of *The Men on the Sixth Floor* was published in 2001, available from The Last Hurrah Bookshop, at <http://members.aol.com/jfkhurrah/>.

11. This extract from Sample and Collom is from David Perry, 'A Few Good Men', at <http.mcadams.posc.mu.edu/goodmentxt> (1995) At that site Perry rubbishes the story in great detail. It isn't difficult to do.

12. 'The identification was made by A. Nathan Darby, a Certified Latent Print Examiner with several decades experience. Mr. Darby signed a sworn, notarised affidavit stating that he was able to affirm a 14-point match between the "Unknown" finger-

print and the "blind" print card submitted to him, which was the 1951 print of Mac Wallace's. US law requires a 12-point match for legal identification; Darby's match is more conclusive than the legal minimum.' From <http://home.earthlink.net/~sixthfloor/prints2.htm>.

13. It cannot be put any more firmly than this. Other possibilities exist, for example that the unidentified print or the Wallace print had been planted. This seems deeply implausible to me. If the Wallace print had been planted in the 'sniper's nest' to falsely implicate him, why not leave it on a rifle, where it might survive and be spotted, rather than a cardboard box, where it might be missed?

14. <http://spot.acorn.net/jfkplace/09/fp.back_issues/22nd_Issue/breakthru2.html>.

15. Robert A. Caro, *The Years of Lyndon Johnson: Volume 1, The Path to Power* (London: Collins, 1982); *Volume 2, Means of Ascent* (London: The Bodley Head, 1990).

16. In that election a box containing a precinct's worth of votes, precinct 13, was never opened. Lyndon's allies in local organised crime had it stuffed full of illegal votes if he needed them. In the event he won without opening it. But his opponent went to court to try and get it opened. It never was. This event became immortalised when it was used in an American TV game show which was eventually imported, unchanged, into the UK in the 1950s as *Take Your Pick*. At the climax of the show the winning

contestant was given the choice of taking the money or 'opening the box' for the surprise prize. The surprise prize was always in box 13. The box was opened with 'the key to box 13'. In Caro's *Means of Ascent* (see note 15) there is a picture of 'box 13', being guarded by some Texas heavies, on p. 286.

17. *Dallas Morning News*, 24 March 1984, quoted by Sample and Collom pp. 122–4. See also J. Evetts Haley, *A Texan Looks at Lyndon* (Canyon, Texas; Palo Duro Press, 1964) pp. 136/7. Haley was a writer, a rancher and a Texas politician, who ran for governor in 1956. On the cover he calls himself 'a life-long Constitutional Democrat'. This means he was a so-called Dixiecrat, the white, Southern, mostly racist members of the uneasy coalition which makes up the Democratic Party. The same group produced Governor George Wallace a few years later. Wallace seemed to be about to impede Richard Nixon's reelection in the 1972 election when Wallace got shot and was paralysed from the waist down by another 'lone assassin'. Though Haley's book describes the scandals around Johnson in the 1960s, nearly as much space is taken up attacking Lyndon for being a lefty new dealer, who '...dismissed the Southern ideals, traditions and memories – bought with Southern fortune, suffering and seas of blood – with obscene and ruthless cruelty. With implications of inter-marriage and a miscengenated race...' Haley p. 228.

18. Robert Winter-Berger, *The Washington Pay-off* (New York: Dell, 1972) pp. 62–63.

19. A third scandal, involving the contract to build a plane, the TFX fighter, was also brewing. A Congressional hearing on the case was scheduled for 27 November but after the assassination on 22 November the committee never met again and those of LBJ's circle involved kept their mouths shut.

20. Haley pp. 107–8. Those are Haley's inverted commas round 'economist'.

21. <http://home.earthlink.net/~sixthfloor/estes. htm>. Estes' allegations about LBJ and the Marshall killing are from the front page of the *Dallas Morning News*, 23 March 1984, quoted by Sample and Collom pp. 112/3.

22. <http://home.earthlink.net/~sixthfloor/estes. htm>. Douglas Caddy discusses this in an interview at <www.spartacus.schoolnet.co.uk/JFKcaddyD. htm>.

23. Reading the letter now it is obvious that the Justice Department would not go anywhere near such an explosive set of allegations and it is difficult to believe that Estes' lawyer wouldn't know this. Estes appears to have talked about this on the record only twice, once to a French magazine *VSD*. I e-mailed *VSD* about getting a copy of the article but they replied that they didn't have copies that far back. However, an account of the Estes interview was at

<http://www.infowar.com/iwftp/cloaks/99/CD _1999–88.txt>. This is the text at that site.

Mon, 26 Apr 1999 18:58:59 +0200
From:
Subject: JFK/BSE/VSD
The following is only a rough sum-up of the Article from VSD, but enough to give our readers the drift of the article.

In the article Billie Sol Estes says that the killing of JFK was decided by Cliff Carter, one of Johnson's cronies and Johnson, himself. Their close associate, one Malcom 'Mack' E. Wallace was charged with the practical aspects of the job. Wallace already had killed in cold blood a friend of the sister of Lyndon, found guilty and condemned to 5 years in prison, a sentence that was suspended! His lawyer, John Cofer was also Lyndon's. In 1963 Wallace recruited Jack Ruby and Lee Harvey Oswald. And Wallace was one of the assassins who shot at JFK. When asked for his proof, he says he got 'the best life insurance I could get… I recorded systematically all my conversations with Wallace, Carter and Johnson'. He also has recording of his conversations with Cliff Carter which evokes the death of JFK. Certain were recorded in Sept. 1963, before the crime, some afterwards.

Asked if he has tapes of Johnson speaking about killing JFK, he answers, 'yes'. 'He said something like, now we have to get rid of that asshole Irishman. Lyndon never went into details, he had Carter attend to that.' He is then asked why he doesn't make the tapes public and he says he will, but first has to have some sort of guarantee for himself and his family. After saying how much the USGVT would want these tapes, etc, he ends by saying: 'I have the solution of the death of JFK. The truth will break open one day.'

The article goes on with 'proof' that 'Mack' Wallace was one of the shooters, that his fingerprints were found on one of the book cartons in the room in the Texas Book School Depository where Oswald was said to do the shooting. Malcom Wallace was killed under strange circumstances in a road accident in 1971. His car was going at very high speeds and hit an electric pylon for no apparent reason. The article is spread over 8 pages and has lots of photographs.'

Subsequently a book was published in France, *Le Dernier Temoin* (The Last Witness) in which Estes gave extended interviews to another French journalist. I have a copy but my French isn't good enough to read it and no English translation appears to exist.

A very good, detailed summary of the state of play on the Wallace/Estes story by Larry Hancock is at <http://educationforum.ipbhost.com/index. php? showtopic =2321>.

24. Haley's book was available in 2002 at <http://www.assassinationweb.com/eb3.htm>. If they don't have it try The Last Hurrah Book shop, for example, which is on the Web at <http://members.aol.com/jfkhurrah/> or <www.abebooks.com/>.

25. These quotes are from <http://users.crocker.com/~acacia/meeting.html>. She died on 22 June 2002. I haven't read her book which is not in the British library system. If the quote is accurate, and we accept that LBJ was behind the shooting in Dallas, it could be read as suggesting he expected Kennedy and Yarborough to be killed the next day. Texas senator Yarborough and Johnson's ally, Governor John Connally, were then involved in a big struggle for control of the Texas Democratic Party. Indeed, that struggle was part of the reason JFK went to Texas: Yarborough was seen by LBJ as a 'Kennedy man' and JFK went there to try to end the conflict. Tenuous though this is, were Yarborough meant to be killed, Connally's famous comment on being hit, 'They're going to kill us all', takes on a new meaning. Was Yarborough meant to be sitting where Connally was? Some reports have claimed that he was, that there was a row at the beginning of the motorcade over seating arrangements.

26. See <http://educationforum.ipbhost.com/lofiversion/index.php/t565.html>.

27. Sample and Collom p. 92. It is of some historical

curiosity that Wallace was the nephew of Roosevelt's vice president, Henry Wallace.

28. Sample and Collom p. 152.

29. <http://63.74.13.36/postp197887.html>.

30. 'The Last Confessions of E. Howard Hunt' <www.rollingstone.com/politics/story/1389314/the_last_confessions_of_e_howard_hunt/8>.

31. Martin Shackelford's critical 1996 comments on the book are at <http://www.acorn.net/jfkplace/03/MS/6th-men.html>. But Shackelford, like Frewin in note 10, was unaware of the significance of the Wallace identification at the time.

32. The biggest display of them is in Robert Groden, *The Search for Lee Harvey Oswald* (London: Bloomsbury, 1995) pp. 247–9. Groden includes several I had never seen before which are much clearer than the two shots reproduced in most of the books.

33. This, curiously enough, was the only book on the case I read in the 1960s. All I can remember of it is an account of Johnson's millions.

Beyond Whodunnit?

Oswald? Which Oswald?

In the previous chapter I skipped over some of the obvious difficulties with Loy Factor's story. In addition to Wallace and a young Hispanic woman, Factor named Oswald and Jack Ruby as being part of the conspiracy: Oswald as a shooter and Ruby as part of the organising team. Given his known activities around the assassination on the day, Ruby's alleged role looks plausible. But Oswald? When Sample and Collom interviewed Factor they knew so little about the case they didn't seem to know that Oswald's putative role in the shooting had been refuted by the buffs over 25 years before them and they didn't think to challenge Factor on his claim that Oswald was on the sixth floor of the book depository. Oswald denied shooting and, not only is there no evidence that he did, voice stress analysis of the tapes of his recorded comments while in custody suggests he is telling the truth.[1]

Factor's account is internally implausible[2] and would be easy to dismiss were it not for his identification of the man called 'Wallace' to Mark Collom in 1971. It is possible that Factor simply added Oswald's name and Ruby's name to his story because those were the names he knew from the media. But in a sense, asking, 'Was Oswald on the sixth floor?' is premature. Before we can discuss *this* we have to answer the question 'Which Oswald?' Because, wacky though this may sound, there seems to have been more than one 'Oswald'.

There is a big book about Oswald by Robert Groden, *The Search for Lee Harvey Oswald* (London: Bloomsbury, 1995), which contains all the extant photographs of him. On the title page there is a *montage* of head shots of Oswald, 19 in all, and they appear to me to show two people. They are similar but not identical and US official records of Oswald appear to show two people of different heights with different scars.[3]

Oswald's biography is still partly a mystery and one of the oldest themes in it has been the idea of a second 'Oswald'. The early critics of the Warren Commission report had noticed that Oswald seemed to be in two places at once at various times in 1963: a second 'Oswald' seemed to be around, drawing attention to himself as a right-wing, anti-Castro agitator, offering to shoot Castro etc.[4] This second, phoney 'Oswald' became part of the theories constructed by the early Warren Report critics, his actions perceived to be part of a plot to set up and frame the real Oswald. Professor Richard Popkin detailed this first in his *The Second Oswald* (London: Andre Deutsch/Sphere, 1967). A decade after

Popkin, the English writer and solicitor, the late Michael Eddowes, published *The Oswald File* (New York: Clarkson Potter, 1977). Eddowes had spotted that there were two Oswalds in the photographs. He had noticed, as had others, that, according to official records, the two Oswalds were not the same height and they had different scars. He concluded that one, the American, the Marine Oswald, went to the Soviet Union but another 'Oswald' came back in his place – a ringer being run by the Soviets, who then shot the president.

In their *Alias Oswald* (Manchester, Maine: GKG Partners, 1985) Robert Cutler and WR Morris argued that the double, the second 'Oswald', was not a Soviet spy but a US spy – real name probably Alec (AJ) Hiddell, this being one of the aliases used by Oswald. In their analysis the switch from one 'Oswald' to the other took place in 1958 while Oswald was serving in the Marine Corps in Japan.

> Serving with his radar unit overseas in Japan, he turns out to be the look-alike of a CIA recruit training for a spy mission to Moscow. The Oswald name, ID, civilian and military background are transferred to the spy.[5]

The Eddowes and Cutler/Morris books are hard work to read: detailed and intricate, with long sequences of claims of the form 'Assuming x, then y and then z', which are both difficult to follow and of little evidential value. But they are merely an appetiser for the most recent version of the 'two Oswalds' thesis by John Armstrong. For some years Armstrong's research was written about by JFK buffs as 'the Armstrong research'; he presented bits of it at conferences and eventually some of these lectures found their way onto the Net. Finally, in 2003 the book arrived, *Harvey and Lee: How the CIA Framed Oswald*.[6]

This is a staggering piece of research, 12 years of it, and a lot of money spent in the process. Armstrong has interviewed people who hadn't been interviewed since the Warren Commission – and some who had never been interviewed before. He has been through areas of the national archives never investigated before, and read official files no non-official had hitherto seen. Lots of new ground is broken here in all kinds of little subsections of the story. Armstrong is a wonderful sleuth. But the book is far too long, the text is full of stupid little errors and the typesetting is eccentric – the text is covered in italicisation, bold and underlining. A great 400- or 500-page book is buried in this 1,200-page monster. Simultaneously grandiose and sloppy, Armstrong's book exemplifies all the faults of self-publication.

Nonetheless he *is* a great sleuth and, by dint of minute examination of the paper record and a lot of phone-bashing and travelling, Armstrong validates part of the Cutler-Morris thesis: there was a switch by the CIA. Or, rather, something more subtle than that happened. Here is Armstrong's version of his basic thesis from one of his lectures:

In the early 1950s an intelligence operation was underway that involved two teenage boys: Lee Oswald, from Fort Worth and a Russian-speaking boy who was given the name 'Harvey Oswald', from New York. Beginning in 1952, these boys lived parallel but separate lives, often in the same city. The ultimate goal was to switch their identities and send Harvey Oswald into Russia, which is exactly what happened, 7 years later.

Lee and Harvey attended different schools, worked at different companies, and lived in different cities. When the Warren Commission pieced together 'Lee Harvey Oswald's' life, they often found evidence of Oswald in two places at the same time. Unable to explain these conflicts, they withheld it from their report. This evidence is the key to understanding the lives of Harvey and Lee Oswald.'[7]

Armstrong set himself the task of nothing less than untangling the intertwined lives of Harvey and Lee. In two senses, this is a fantastic idea. From the viewpoint of – say – the editor of *History Today*, Armstrong's thesis about such an intelligence operation is a fantastic idea in the sense of implausible, preposterous. But that's the view from outside the JFK research world. Inside the world of JFK buffs, it is a fantastic idea because it is so perfect, because it is such a beautiful idea which rings with the pure, true tones of elegance and sophistication that you sometimes get from a good theory. Whether true or false, this is a huge idea in the JFK assassination world.

To get a handle on this we have to go back to the early

1950s, some of the cooler years of the Cold War. The US had no reliable information on the Soviet Union. (This was before U-2 over-flights and spy-satellites.) Soviet missiles, nuclear weapons, even the Soviet economy, were largely a mystery. The agents sent in by CIA and MI6 in the early Cold War years, mostly anti-communist émigrés, had been turned or captured. Formal diplomatic contacts with the Soviet bloc were totally constrained: all Western visitors were followed and monitored, and large areas of the Soviet bloc were off-limits to visitors. There really was an Iron Curtain, which presented the most acute difficulties to the Western intelligence services. How could they get agents in? One way was to send them in as defectors.[8] Over the last 20 years it has emerged in fragments that there was a CIA programme of sending apparent defectors to the USSR.[9] Armstrong discusses some of these. We have never had any positive evidence of this operation working; no leaks about deception operations or useful information gathered. Maybe they all failed.[10]

Armstrong believes that there was an attempt at a smarter defection. Armstrong believes the CIA ran two real identities in parallel, merged them – Lee and Harvey became Lee Harvey – and switched them just before the apparent defection of the American 'Oswald', Lee. In went Harvey pretending to be Lee. Thus the CIA would insert into the Soviet Union a defector, Harvey, with two outstanding characteristics: one, unknown to the Soviet authorities, he could speak fluent Russian and two, when Soviet intelligence checked Lee Oswald's biography, as the CIA presumed they would, they would find the American 'Lee Oswald', not an intelligence cover story, a 'legend', but a real life – the ultimate 'legend'. If this seems elaborate, Armstrong reminds the reader of Soviet intelligence's use of 'illegals', and quotes the example of Molody, 'Gordon Lonsdale', who operated in the UK for many years.

This hypothesised CIA plan entailed both boys being in the Marines at the same time. Armstrong shows reports and presents recollections of 'Oswald' in two places at the same time through secondary school and in the Marines. The theory of two 'Oswalds' explains the contradictory material about Oswald in the Marines: one Oswald who couldn't shoot, one who could: one who was an apparent Marxist and read Russian, the other who didn't: one who was outgoing and a brawler, the other a bookworm. Comparing the calm, rational, mild Oswald who did the radio interview in New Orleans and made the distinction between being a Marxist and being a fan of the Soviet Union, with the reports of the gung-ho, would-be assassin of Castro – is this really the same person? Armstrong's 'two Oswalds' thesis makes a kind of immediate sense when you consider the wildly contrasting behaviour and beliefs attributed to 'Oswald'.[11]

It should be noted that there is no evidence, either paper record or first-hand, that this scheme took place. Armstrong infers it from the evidence of the existence of the two 'Oswalds'. If this is true, Armstrong has uncovered a most elaborate intelligence operation (this is really a rather impressive wheeze), and done the greatest piece of espionage detective work I have ever read about.[12]

Into the CIA's Anti-Castro Underground

In Armstrong's thesis, after Russian-speaking 'Harvey' defected, adopting American 'Lee's' identity, 'Lee' Oswald remained in the US, disappearing into the CIA-funded, anti-Castro world of spies and military training. Armstrong traces 'Lee' by collecting all the reports of 'Lee Harvey Oswald' which did not fit the official, Warren Commission biography of Oswald, anomalous sightings, collected by the FBI and police. Armstrong follows the American, anti-Castro activist Lee Oswald through his role in framing Harvey Oswald, right up to a late night meeting in a cafe with Jack Ruby on 21 November 1963 and into the book depository. Armstrong offers the revision of all revisions: *two 'Oswalds' in the book depository*. One, the American Lee, was on the sixth floor with another man, helping to frame the other, Harvey, who worked there. (Armstrong doesn't quite say that Lee fired from the sixth floor but it is implicit that he or the unidentified other man did.)

Some of this is convincing and some less so. For the biography of the American, Lee, and particularly for the later events close to the assassination, Armstrong relies almost entirely on eyewitnesses, and eyewitnesses are generally not reliable. However, he has many of them all saying roughly the same thing: can they all be mistaken?[13]

LBJ and Hoover

The major initial proponents of the 'lone assassin' story in Washington were President Johnson and those around him and the FBI.[14] Johnson prevented Congress and the Senate from holding hearings into the assassination, and prevented Texas state authorities from pursuing a criminal investigation. (See chapter 2.) The FBI took control of the investigation, had all the evidence collected by the Dallas police flown to Washington and 'edited' it – removed, altered or fabricated hundreds of items – to make it fit the predetermined 'lone assassin' verdict.

We don't know what specific motive Hoover had – if any – beyond the FBI's general embarrassment at not preventing the assassination nor if he personally, or the Bureau collectively, had any knowledge of the LBJ-instigated assassination.[15] In his *Act of Treason* (New York: Carroll and Graf, 1991), Mark North claimed that Hoover was warned in 1962 of an assassination plot being hatched by Mafia leader Carlos Marcello and did nothing.[16] But while it is true that at least two reports of a Mob plot were made to FBI agents, there is nothing specifically linking this to Hoover.[17] In the references in the North book's index to 'Hoover: knowledge of Mafia contract on JFK', there is no *evidence* that Hoover knew of the alleged plot. There is a lot of surmise taking the form 'since X knew, then Hoover must have been told'.

Did LBJ tell Hoover of the plot? Would LBJ need to square the Bureau before going ahead? We don't know. For Tony Frewin, with whom I have discussed JFK for over 20 years, it is not credible that a little Texas gang would do something on this scale without clearing it in some way with the powers-that-be.[18] I'm not so sure. The Johnson group planned to leave a crime *and* its solution: a dead Oswald would be served up. Would there have been much federal involvement in an open and shut case? Might Johnson not have calculated that, as the new president, he would be able to handle Hoover – who would, in any case, be delighted to see the demise of the Kennedys?

LBJ and Hoover had been allies of a kind for many years. Hoover had used the FBI to vet employees at LBJ's radio station; they were neighbours for 19 years in Washington and walked their dogs together[19]; and Johnson had lobbied to ensure a good deal for Hoover should he have to retire at the end of the Eisenhower administration. In the event he didn't.[20] They also had friends in common, notably the Texas oil man, Clint Murchison. Letters exchanged between Hoover and LBJ, reproduced in Mark North's *Act of Treason* between pages 352–3 and in Appendix A, show how friendly they were – on the surface at least. And they both detested the Kennedy brothers. Just as JFK's death saved Johnson from prosecution and disgrace, so it probably extended Hoover's career. For the Kennedy brothers had longed to rid themselves of him and they might have tried to do so had JFK been re-elected in 1964. Given the amount of dirt Hoover had on John Kennedy's sexual activities going back to the 1940s, whether or not they would have succeeded is a different matter.

Our understanding of the FBI cover-up in the immediate aftermath of the shooting has been massively expanded by the research of John Armstrong in the National Archives. He has documented in extraordinary detail how the FBI 'edited' the evidence it had. Armstrong believes that the material in the FBI's possession was edited by them *in an attempt to remove evidence of the two Oswalds.* This might be true but there are two other possible explanations of their behaviour. First, the FBI may have edited out all the anomalous material because they didn't want anomalies appearing in what they had accepted as the necessary, official explanation of the dreadful deed. Second, the FBI may have edited out the anomalous material because, as professional investigators, they were used to getting such material in investigations – the human memory is none too reliable – and disregarded it as a matter of course.

Armstrong's basic thesis appeared in a two part article in the now defunct magazine *Probe*, September-October and November-December 1997, 22 pages in all, something in the region of 15,000 words. A version of this long essay, a transcription of a lecture Armstrong gave, is on the web[21] and these quotes will give a flavour of it. References in brackets are to slide projections Armstrong used in his lecture.

> The #5 man in the FBI, William Sullivan, said (RIGHT-SLIDE 70) 'Hoover did not like to see the Warren Commission come into existence. He showed a marked interest in limiting the scope of it and taking any action which might result in neutralising it.' (RIGHT-SLIDE 71). If there were documents that possibly he didn't want to come to the light of the public, then those documents no longer exist, and the truth will never be known. All FBI reports were first sent to FBI headquarters in Washington for analysis before being passed on to the Warren Commission. Testimony that conflicted with the FBI's written report or hinted of a conspiracy was dealt with in several ways: (LEFT-SLIDE 73) testimony was either 1) suppressed 2) ignored 3) fabricated 4) altered or 5) destroyed.
>
> Testimony that was suppressed included records that were withheld from the public or not published by the Warren Commission. Suppressed records include the FBI's report concerning the woman who knew Oswald's father and uncle in New York City, FBI reports that placed Oswald in two different locations at the same time, such as those from North Dakota and New York, the US and Japan, Russia and the US, and in New Orleans and Dallas – all at the same time. Laurel Kitrell's 30 page statement concerning the two Oswalds was suppressed. Numerous FBI reports of a 2nd Oswald preceding the assassination and statements of people who reported Oswald and Jack Ruby together were suppressed... Testimony that was

ignored includes the statements of Palmer McBride, Walter Gehrke, witnesses who saw Oswald and Ruby together, and witnesses who saw Oswald drive a car. Dr. Milton Kurian, who interviewed a very small, malnourished (Harvey) Oswald in New York, was ignored. Allen Felde told the FBI he was with (Harvey) Oswald in Memphis, when (Lee) Oswald was supposed to be in Japan. The FBI ignored Felde and failed to interview other Marines stationed in Memphis in order to determine whether Oswald was in Memphis or Japan or in both locations at the same time. The FBI interviewed twenty eight Marines who knew Russian-speaking Harvey in Santa Anna, California in 1959. But they ignored the statements of Marines who were stationed with Lee Oswald at the Marine Corps air station in El Toro, California at the same time. FBI agents became suspicious and began to comment on how unusual the investigation was because no agent was allowed to pursue any kind of a lead to its logical conclusion. Failing to follow through on productive leads suggests that someone was controlling the investigation and leery of placing new information on record which would conflict with the FBI's already completed report... Ray Carney told FBI agents he met with Oswald on five occasions at the airport in Garland, Texas, in May of 1961. The agents told Carney that Oswald was in Russia at that time and that he was obviously mistaken. Barber shop owner Cliff Shasteen told the Warren Commission about cutting Oswald's hair in late summer and Oswald driving Ruth Paine's car. FBI Agent Bardwell Odom told Shasteen that his statements contradicted other information. Shasteen told Agent Odum (RIGHT-SLIDE 73) 'I don't care what it contradicts with,

that's just the facts and that's it'. When Palmer McBride
told Air Force Intelligence Officers and FBI agents that he
worked with Oswald in 1957 and 1958 in New Orleans,
it contradicted Oswald's Marine service in Japan at the
same time. To avoid dealing with McBride, the Warren
Commission did not interview him. Instead, they interviewed his friend William Wulf.

And so on and so on. The numerous witnesses and documents which appear to identify two 'Oswalds' going
back to their childhoods are very striking, thoroughly
documented in many instances and, if true, resolve
nearly all of the difficulties created by the various 'two
Oswalds' stories described earlier in this chapter. For
that reason, because it explains a great deal, this is a
good hypothesis.

For the LBJ-dunnit thesis, Armstrong's thesis makes
intelligible Loy Factor's story of his 'Oswald' leaving the
book depository after the shooting, while apparently
being able to be found at the same time in the canteen:
they were different 'Oswalds'.[22]

The Role of the Secret Service

Anyone looking at the actions of the Secret Service in
Dallas that day might wonder how hard they were
trying. L. Fletcher Prouty, who had been in charge of
presidential security in the 1950s, looked at the Secret
Service's actions in Dallas and wondered if they hadn't

been in on the assassination. Where were the guards on roofs with rifles? Why hadn't the buildings on the route been cleared of people? Why did the presidential limousine slow down when the first shot was fired when it should have speeded up?[23] I don't have an answer to those questions but, for no good reason that I could articulate, I could never quite bring myself to believe that the Secret Service had been corrupted. However, an American researcher called Vince Palamara has spent years tracking down and interviewing the Secret Service personnel from that period and has revealed a considerable degree of enmity towards JFK among some of the Secret Service agents. Some of the more conservative and religious among them found his sexual promiscuity repellent and felt that he was besmirching the presidency – a view undoubtedly shared by J. Edgar Hoover. Palamara hasn't proved that the Secret Service were privy to the assassination conspiracy but he has made that a much less implausible idea.[24]

Two 'Oswalds' and Two 'JFKs'?

In chapter 4 I commented on the still unresolved conflict between the account of Kennedy's wounds given by the doctors who first treated him in the emergency room at Parkland Hospital and the account in the autopsy. This is at the heart of the quagmire which is now the medical/forensic evidence.[25] The problem can be seen at a glance if you go to the search engine Google, click on 'images' on its opening display and then ask it for 'JFK autopsy pictures'. On the first couple of pages you are shown both a colour picture showing the back of Kennedy's head as a clotted mass of blood and brains and his right temple intact *and* a black and white picture showing the back of the head in pristine condition (and in the uncropped version, with a big hole in his right temple). One of the pictures must be a fabrication – *or they are pictures of two different heads*. This simple but exhilarating idea comes from Robert Morningstar's 'The Ultimate Secret of the Assassination'.[26] Morningstar isn't a writer, can't punctuate and hadn't bothered to have his site proofread by anyone who can do these things when I looked at it. He is an eccentric: in his introduction he tells us that in 1997 he was elected 'Presider (sic) of the Ancient Druid Order of England' and opens his account thus:

> For 35 years, the world has wondered about the circumstances surrounding the John F. Kennedy Assassination. The facts of the case lay in murky darkness mired, like a body sunken in a bog awaiting resurrection or revival.
>
> For 35 years, having been a witness to these historical events, I have collected the facts surrounding that singular moment in our dark history in the hope of someday bringing the truth to light. I did this for one reason and one person only. The quest has lead me across continents and oceans, even back to Camelot. I have descended into the underworld. I have communed with the dead. I have drawn the Sword from the Stone to redeem the soul and restore the body of a Celtic king to his rightful place. The

journey is dangerous but the reward is to arrive one day out of darkness into light. WARNING: AN AMERICAN GOTHIC HORROR.

All that notwithstanding, Morningstar has done something very striking. Like others, Morningstar was thinking about the conflict between the account of the wounds given by the Parkland doctors and that given at the autopsy. He discovered that JD Tippit, the police officer also shot that day, allegedly by Oswald, and John F. Kennedy looked similar enough for Tippit to be have been nicknamed 'JFK' by some of his Dallas police colleagues. *He shows pictures; there is a striking similarity.* He also noticed that the wounds suffered by Tippit were similar to the wounds described by the JFK autopsy surgeons. *He shows more pictures.* He gives the reader a great deal of complicated analysis of skulls, faces, marks, blemishes – *many more pictures* – some of which I followed, some I didn't. (As with all the medical evidence in the case, a good deal of anatomical and medical knowledge is required.) He suggests that the conflict between the Parkland doctors and the autopsy surgeons is explicable: the 'JFK autopsy' was carried out on Tippit, not JFK. So the pictures displayed by Google as JFK autopsy pictures are actually pictures of both JFK (in colour, back of head clotted blood and brains) *and* Tippit (black and white, rear of head intact). Thus, argues Morningstar, it is Tippit's body which is in JFK's grave in the Arlington Cemetery.

This scenario is just feasible but it raises nearly as

many difficulties as David Lifton's corpse-altering theory in *Best Evidence*. Assuming, as does Morningstar, that the switch was deliberate, who did it? Who decided to do it? When was the decision made? Two autopsies were carried out, though we know little about the second one.[27] If we reject Lifton's wound-altering explanation, Morningstar's hypothesis is the only one which reconciles the conflicts between the Parkland doctors and the autopsy. Thus far, to my knowledge, none of the forensic experts in the field have deigned to comment on Morningstar's beguiling thesis.

Conclusion: or Where are the Historians?

Even a casual glance at academic accounts of America in the 1960s shows that historians either avoid trying to deal with the assassination of Kennedy (and those of Robert Kennedy and King), or they simply present the official verdict without comment, as if it was unproblematic. This isn't terribly surprising: it is impossible to accommodate the reality of the assassinations of the 1960s within a safe, academic, pluralist perspective. So historians of America have reached a tacit understanding to give themselves a dispensation: we need not bother with this. And they don't. This is from a long essay on this issue by David Mantik.

> Inasmuch as the assassination is a major event of the twentieth century, and may well represent a turning point in

American history, it is incumbent upon historians to understand and explain this event – as well as those that surround it. To date, however, a deafening silence has reigned on these matters, as historians have preferred to tolerate the harvest of The Warren Report rather than to cultivate their own fields.

Possibly inquisitive historians, naturally enough, have no craving to be tainted as barmy by the media paintbrushes, as well might befall them were they to admit publicly to such curiosity. The plain fact, though, is that this controversial issue frightens historians: most genuinely fear for their own professional prestige, and many fear subconsciously at what would gaze back at them from the subterranean depths of this case were they to peer too intently into the well of history. Given the unique nature of these events, and their profound impact on America, this fear is understandable. Ultimately, however, these issues must be faced honestly and responsibly. It is no longer sufficient merely to quote a lawyer turned journalist on these serious questions, nor can the matter be left to the most amateur of professions – the media... Heretofore, the historians' tacitly donned mantle of innocence radiated an aura of genteel credibility, but that mantle has become threadbare. If historians continue to deny the deceitful reality underlying the post-assassination cover-up, they, too, risk becoming accessories after the fact.[28]

'Accessories after the fact' is a little harsh. There are all manner of good reasons for historians – and academics in general – to stay away from the Kennedy assassination. Not least is the danger of being contaminated by the conspiracy theories which are draped all over the subject. There is nothing an academic wants less than to be tarred with the conspiracy theorist brush; this is the kiss of death, the intellectual black spot. Academics, and historians in particular, will continue to avoid the subject: it has nothing to offer them except possible embarrassment. American politicians will continue to avoid the subject until they find some way of using it to their advantage and none seems obvious. Which more or less leaves the position as it was in 1964 with groups of individuals trying to make sense of it.

At present the Kennedy assassination research community has not accepted the Johnson-Wallace solution to the case. Indeed, if what is on the Net is anything to go by, most of that group is only just becoming aware of the thesis and there will be considerable resistance to the idea. JFK researchers are just like other people and don't like having to ditch old theories for new ones. But even if it is eventually accepted, there are still huge unresolved areas in which the research will continue. If your field is forensics, say, or the medical evidence, or, like Vincent Palamara mentioned above, the Secret Service, it is virtually irrelevant who pulled the trigger or gave the order to do so. The show will go on.

The show will go on but the house rules have changed. With very little attention from the major media, something like a third official inquiry into the assassination took place in the 1990s. Following the enormous publicity generated by Oliver Stone's film, *JFK*, in 1992 the Assassination Archives Review Board

(AARB) was created by Congress. The Board's chair remarked on its unique nature:

> First, the Congress established the Review Board as an independent agency outside of the controls of the agencies maintaining records. Second, the Board consisted of five citizens, trained in law, history, and archives, who were not federal employees but who had the ability to order agencies to declassify government documents – the first time in history that an outside group had such power. Third, the standards to be applied by the Board strongly favored disclosure. All records were *presumed* to be immediately disclosed, and the Board could protect information only if the agency proved by 'clear and convincing evidence' that the harm of disclosure outweighed the *public's interest* in the information. And fourth, and perhaps most important, once the Board made a decision that a document should be declassified, only the President could overrule its decision. The structural and practical independence created by the Congress was essential for the Review Board to meet the anticipated pressure to keep records secret, particularly intelligence and law enforcement documents.[29]

From 1994–98 the AARB briefed American historians, held hearings, took advice on what to look for from the JFK researchers, and produced another mountain of documents which have been transferred to the National Archives. This enormous cache of new material will take years – decades, perhaps – be to be processed.[30]

The show will go on.

Notes

1. A former CIA officer, George O'Toole, used voice stress analysis equipment on the various fragments of recordings of Oswald made that day in the Dallas police station. See his *The Assassination Tapes: An Electronic Probe into the Murder of John F. Kennedy and the Dallas Cover up* (New York: Penthouse Press, 1975) which began as an article in the July 1973 issue of *Penthouse*.

2. See note 11 in the previous chapter.

3. See Groden pp. 240–250 for a summary. There is a detailed analysis of the varying recorded heights of 'Oswald' in Michael Eddowes, *The Oswald File* (New York: Clarkson Potter, 1977). Appendix D.

4. Most conspicuous was the man identified by the CIA as 'Lee Harvey Oswald' who was photographed outside the Soviet embassy in Mexico City. See Groden (note 10) pp. 247–9 for the best collection of these photographs. This is discussed at the end of the previous chapter.

5 Cutler and Morris p. xii.

6. Arlington, Texas: Quasar Ltd., 2003 $40, plus postage, from <www.jfkresearch.com/armstrong/>. There is an account of one of his early lectures at the 1997 JFK Lancer annual conference at <www.jfklancer.com/KWinter97-2.html> which conveys both a sense of the content of Armstrong's research and the excitement it caused among some

American JFK researchers.

7. <www.enteract.com/-hargrove/Dakota/Harvey-Dakota.htm>.

8. The Soviets were doing the same thing, sending a stream of bogus defectors to the West, trying to disinform and penetrate the NATO intelligence agencies. The recent book by former CIA officer, Tennent H. Bagley, *Spy Wars* (London: Yale University Press, 2007) is almost entirely about the problems caused to CIA counterintelligence by the stream of defectors from the Soviet bloc. This is the 'wilderness of mirrors' associated with the former head of CIA counterintelligence James Angleton, orchid-grower, poetry-writer – almost the only glamorous figure in the post-war intelligence story.

9. A phoney defection was the plot of the most famous British spy novel/film of the period, John Le Carré's *The Spy Who Came in From the Cold*.

10. See <www.ctka.net/pr397–otepka.html> for a discussion of this which suggests how closely guarded were the programme's secrets: in the case under discussion here, it ended the career of a senior State Department official who got curious about it.

11. The plan also meant two 'mothers of Oswald', two 'Marguerite Oswalds'. If Armstrong is correct, and the evidence looks convincing, a woman spent nearly ten years, pretending to be 'Marguerite Oswald'. It isn't clear if the 'mother' of Harvey, the

Russian-speaker, was actually his mother or an intelligence officer playing the role.

12. Was the 'two Oswalds' defection scheme the only one of its kind or merely an example of a wider operation involving other ID switches? If the latter, no other evidence has been uncovered thus far.

13. A serious-minded sceptic would say 'yes' to that question. Armstrong quotes people remembering what Oswald's mother looked like nearly 40 years before. Can you remember what a neighbour looked like 30 or 40 years ago? Armstrong's earlier version of his 'two Oswalds' thesis is attacked at <http://mcadams.posc.mu.edu/2oswalds.htm>. For a more sympathetic review, one which grasps the enormity of what Armstrong has attempted, *Harvey and Lee* is reviewed by Walt Brown at <www.jfkresearch.com/critique/critique-view.html>. Brown notes all the errors and the lack of copy editing but sees beyond that to the extraordinary work Armstrong has done.

14. This is discussed in Larry Hancock's recent *Someone Would Have Talked* (Texas: Lancer Productions, 2006).

15. There is one strange book, Michael Milan, *The Squad: The US Government's Secret Alliance With Organized Crime* (London: Prion, 1989) in which the pseudonymous author describes his role in a squad of gangsters recruited by J. Edgar Hoover in 1947 to do dirty work for the FBI. Milan describes killing a taxi driver in Dallas on the day after the assassina-

tion. (The taxi driver apparently had some role in the shooting.) Milan returns to Washington to meet J. Edgar Hoover who says, 'You already know too much. So I'll just say: Johnson. No doubt. We stand away.' (p. 210) No-one in the JFK assassination research community has taken Milan's book seriously and I see no reason to do so. Still, for the period, it was a very striking reference to Hoover/Johnson.

16. Mark North, *Act of Treason*, (New York: Carroll and Graf, 1991).

17. Anthony Summers, *Official and Confidential: The Secret Life of J. Edgar Hoover* (London: Gollancz, 1993) pp. 325–328.

18. Tony (Anthony) Frewin wrote *The Assassination of John F. Kennedy: An Annotated Film, TV, and Videography, 1963–92* (London: Greenwood Press, 1993).

19. Mark North, *Act of Treason* (New York: Carroll and Graf, 1991) p. 52.

   There is a good deal of fragmented information on the Hoover-Johnson relationship in Summers (see note 17 above), Athan Theoharis and John Stuart Cox, *The Boss* (London: Harrap, 1989) and Curt Gentry, *J. Edgar Hoover: The Man and the Secrets* (London: Norton, 1991).

20. Anthony Summers, *Official and Confidential: The Secret Life of J. Edgar Hoover* (London: Gollancz 1993) p. 263.

21. <www.enteract.com/-hargrove/Dakota/Harvey-

Dakota.htm>.

22. Armstrong's two 'Oswalds' thesis has not gone unchallenged. For example at <http://mcadams. posc.mu.edu/2oswalds.htm> Armstrong's claims are critiqued and the anonymous author concludes:

> So is there nothing at all to the "two Oswalds" theories? No, nothing at all. The whole rickety structure is built on unreliable witness testimony, carefully selected and inaccurate documents, and a mountain of implausible supposition. Which makes it a fitting metaphor for JFK assassination conspiracy theories generally.

This dismissive verdict is premature: the analysis which precedes it does not deal with all the evidence Armstrong had brought forward (there is even more now in the book and this critique was pre-book publication). But it does raise questions about Armstrong's thesis. Armstrong does depend heavily on eyewitness testimony and that is notoriously unreliable. It is going to take someone with more patience than I have, and access to the original documents in the archives, to go through Armstrong's work and the points of his critics to resolve this issue.

23. See L. Fletcher Prouty, *JFK* (New York: Birch Lane Press, 1992) pp. 291–294.

24. Palamara's research into the actions of the Secret Service, *Survivor's Guilt: The Secret Service and the*

Failure to Protect the President is now available on the Net at <www.assassinationresearch.com/v4n1.html>

25. Or even *all* the physical evidence. Even the famous Zapruder film is now believed to have been doctored. See part four of James H. Fetzer (ed.) *Assassination Science* (Chicago: Catfeet Press, 1996) and Google for the so-called stabilised version of Zapruder's film which is widely available, e.g. at <http://blogfiles.wfmu.org/KF/0512/zapruder_-_stable.mov>.

In his testimony in 1994 before the Assassination Archives Review Board at <http://mcadams.posc.mu.edu/arrb/index51.htm> the well known JFK researcher, Harrison Livingstone, stated: '… all of the physical evidence in this case was faked.' Of Livingstone's work on the medical evidence Tony Frewin once wrote: 'Harrison Livingstone will make you wish you'd never heard of the medical evidence…'

26. To be found at at <www.jfkresearch.com/morningstar/morningstar3.htm>

27. See <www.washingtonpost.com/wp-srv/national/longterm/jfk/jfk1110.htm>.

28. From David W. Mantik, 'Paradoxes of the JFK Assassination: The Silence of the Historians' at <http://www.harrison-e-livingstone.com/jfk/mantik.htm>

29. 'The Assassination Records Review Board:

Unlocking the Government's Secret Files on the Murder of a President' by John R. Tunheim, from *The Public Lawyer*, Vol. 8, No. 1, Winter 2000, at <http://mcadams.posc.mu.edu/arrb/tunheim.htm>.

30. The final report of the AARB is at <http://www.fas.org/sgp/advisory/arrb98/index.html>. See also <http://www.archives.gov/research_room/jfk/assassination_records_review_board.html>.

Index